Advance praise for *He Heard Me*

"If I didn't already know Christ, I sure would want to after reading this book. We are living in a hurting world; people need to read this, to know there is hope. Truly inspiring!"

—Joanne Cook
Church Treasurer

"This book is very inspiring and would lead me to a relationship with Christ if I didn't have one already."

—Diane Stein
Treasurer
TOPS Woodstock, ON, 1059

He HEARD Me

Brenda Vargas

HE HEARD ME
Copyright © 2016 by Brenda Vargas
Cover photo by Pedro Silva

ISBN: 978-1-4866-1249-9

Word Alive Press
131 Cordite Road, Winnipeg, MB R3W 1S1
www.wordalivepress.ca

RECYCLED
Paper made from
recycled material
FSC® C103567

Library and Archives Canada Cataloguing in Publication

Vargas, Brenda, 1949-, author
    He heard me / Brenda Vargas.

Issued in print and electronic formats.
ISBN 978-1-4866-1249-9 (paperback).--ISBN 978-1-4866-1250-5 (pdf).--
ISBN 978-1-4866-1251-2 (html).--ISBN 978-1-4866-1252-9 (epub)

    1. Christian life. I. Title.

BV4501.3.V37 2016   248.4   C2016-900079-6
                                          C2016-900080-X

This book is dedicated to my husband, Mateus, and to my parents, Orine (Bob) and Joyce Bates.

It is also dedicated to a very special lady, Nancy Chesney, who is truly an example of Christ. She continually shows God's love and compassion to people by praying with them, listening, visiting, and encouraging them with just the right book to read. I am truly blessed to have her as a dear friend in Christ.

Contents

ACKNOWLEDGEMENTS

Lori Nanskeville

Pastor Ian Mills

Geraldine Ross

Nancy Chesney

Joanne Cook

My husband, Mateus

Others who have spoken into my life

Introduction

This book is truly Holy Spirit-directed! I say this because several years ago, not long after accepting Christ as my Lord and Saviour, I started experiencing things in a way I never had before, and I felt the need to journal everything. This book presents some of those journal entries as they were written, along with other uplifting stories about God at work that friends and acquaintances have shared with me.

One morning as I was getting ready for church, I distinctly heard a voice say, "He Heard Me," and with that, I knew the title of the book God was preparing for me to write. I began to work on this book as I was led.

After a few years, I had the opportunity to meet a pastor from London, Ontario. When the actual meeting was over, he told me that earlier in the day he had been praying about our meeting and that God had told him some things about me. He was told that in the book God was giving me to write, not only my poems would appear but much, much more, including God's plans for the book. This amazed me because there was no possible way this pastor could know about my book unless he did, in fact, hear it from God.

As I continue my interesting, rewarding, and sometimes challenging journey with God, I am amazed at how much He loves us in spite of ourselves. To think that the Creator of the Universe looks after every little detail of our lives with love, care, and compassion! He never fails.

How exciting it would be if we did not take things for granted, but realized that what we see, feel, and experience in so many ways is actually God letting us know He is here for us.

I hope that my little story about my walk with a robin will touch your heart, and help you to be sensitive to your surroundings so that you don't miss a visit from God.

Other stories will help show you that nothing is impossible for God, and that His timing is everything.

Above all, don't hesitate to dream big and think big—we serve a big God! He wants the best for us, His children.

So go ahead and say with me, "Don't let the devil steal what God wants to give you."

PURPOSE

I believe this book will accomplish all that God has planned for it, igniting faith in believers at all levels, and awakening their desire to get to know God more. The ultimate goal is that the person reading this book who is searching for meaning and purpose in their life will accept Jesus Christ as their personal Saviour.

Thank You for a Mother's Prayer

Some people like a good romance with a happy ending, while others like to read something that intrigues them. Hopefully, as you begin to read this book, you will find it intriguing and interesting enough to see it to the end. There is no dashing prince or beautiful blonde. There is a main character, who is a man like no other, and there are more people than just one leading lady. There is a hunger and thirst after righteousness, and a love that goes beyond our human comprehension.

Of course, the greatest love story is God proving His love by giving us His only Son to die on the cross for our sins. Hallelujah!

It all started on Thursday, April 29, 1993, when a group of people at a fellowship group in Brockville were led by the Holy Spirit to pray for family members' salvation instead of having their Bible study. My mother was a member of that group.

Just three days after that, Sunday, May 2, I was sitting down by the water relaxing after working all day. I was mesmerized by the warm sun and by how the wind created little waves along the shoreline; it was so beautiful. I couldn't help but tell God how amazing things were—the colours in the trees and the sky—and how wonderful it was to hear the songs of the birds.

Then out of nowhere I heard a voice say, "Tonight you should be in church."

I looked up and asked, "Is that you, Dad, or is that you, God?" You see, my dad died about ten months earlier and I knew he was in heaven. Strangely enough, the last Sunday he was still with us had also been the second day of the month. Anyway, I heard the voice say again, "Tonight you should be in church."

Just as clearly, I heard another voice telling me not to go, that I would miss the sunset and the warm breezes. It reminded me of how hard I had worked that day, and that I deserved to sit here and just enjoy the beauty. However, I also found myself remembering what my friend, Geri, had told me about Eastdale Christian Outreach. Sometimes their minister would be invited to go to speak at another church and some of the congregation would also go to be a part of the service. There was something soft and gentle about the first voice that led me to think it was only concerned about my wellbeing, and with that I decided to go home and phone the church that Geri had told me about. I called it and heard a recording of the times of the services; I remember looking at the floor and saying, "See devil, the church is open."

God loved me so much that He had provided a way for me to hear about the Eastdale Christian Outreach Centre on Alice Street in Woodstock, Ontario. I was selling Mary Kay part-time, plus working my full-time job as Assistant Manager at a service centre on Highway 401. God had given me a desire to have nice-looking nails. Funny how I found out about a certain lady who did nails. I remember putting off calling her, thinking I was just being vain, and yet I could not get rid of my desire to call her. This went on for quite a few months until I finally called and set up an appointment. The lady's name was Geraldine Ross, but she told me, "Just call me Geri." I noticed that she had a few items with scripture verses on them lying on her desk, so I quickly realized that I should watch my language and not tell any dirty jokes around her. I think it was about the second appointment I started to open up about myself.

The atmosphere was peaceful and there was just something about her that made me feel like I could talk to her about different things in the Bible. I told her a little about my background—I believed that God answered prayer, but everything was cool. I felt like I had everything in my life under control and was doing fine. I would ask something about the Bible and she would share a scripture or even an experience. Geri had such a peace about her, and when she talked about how God and the Holy Spirit showed up at Eastdale, she was stirring an interest down in my soul that I did not realize.

I went to Eastdale Christian Outreach Centre that very night after being down by the water. It had such a charged-up atmosphere that I could not get over it. I was nervous being there by myself and was looking around for Geri when I saw another lady I knew through work. We talked, and then Geri saw me and came over to tell me where she was sitting. I joined her, not realizing I would never be the same again.

The music was so different from the songbooks I'd used in the past. The words we sang were more like a love song to Jesus Himself. I noticed that the singers had such contentment about them—their eyes seemed to sparkle, and the praise and worship was so uplifting. The pastor's message was encouraging, funny and exciting.

He closed the sermon with a question like I never heard before, which blew me away. He asked, "If I wrote you a cheque for a thousand dollars, wouldn't you love me and want to do anything for me?" A few of the congregation chuckled and agreed.

He asked the same question again and then added, "Now think of what God has done for you. Shouldn't you love Him and want to do anything for Him?" Well, if that didn't pull at my heart! I had massive butterflies flying around inside of me. He asked for every head to be bowed and every eye closed, and I think that before he had even finished asking his question, I had my hand up and was crying tears of release.

The salvation question is where the pastor asks if anyone would like to ask Jesus into their hearts, to wash away their sins and make them like a brand-new person. If you are hearing about this for the first time, I would encourage you to ask Jesus into your heart; He can wash away sin, heal the broken-hearted, and create in you a new way of living.

Well, I was not used to lifting my hands in the air while singing repetitive songs; I wasn't used to praying in tongues like the congregation did at this church, but I was changed. I remember asking God to make me like Jesus, but not crazy like these people. I repeated that seven times, with tears freely flowing down my face. It seemed that the more I was crying and calling to Him, the more I felt acceptance and love. Someone had picked me up out of the gutter.

I left church that night more changed than I could imagine. A terrific weight had been lifted off my shoulders.

Nothing I had ever done in my whole life made me feel this high, this loved, this happy—or should I say exhilarated?

What is great about this love story is that it continues to get better, and the love has grown deeper with more understanding of just Who it is that loves me so much. He not only loves me, but He has an exciting daily adventure planned for me here on this earth. He also has a fantastic dream for me which He reveals as I search to know Him more. Like any new relationship, you have to spend time with each other and talk. Praying or talking to God is like talking to a friend.

Thank you, God, for leading my mother's Bible group back then into intercessory prayer for family salvation. Thank you, God, for putting in me a desire to know You, and then for speaking to me when I was just enjoying Your beauty. Most of all, God, thank you for loving me so much that You sent Your only Son to die for me and wash away all my sins that I would have eternal life. John 3:16 states, *"For God so loved the world that he gave his one and only Son, that whoever believes in him shall not perish but have eternal life."*

Heart's Door

Thank you Jesus...
For standing at my heart's door
Waiting to give me so much more
If He isn't within you, I implore
Quickly, open your heart's door.
Walking with Him isn't some silly ploy
He will give you love, peace and joy
Oh to seek His warm and wonderful grace
Just look up and focus on that loving face.
Jesus is there through thick and thin
He will take you out of bondage and sin
Ask Jesus in, He'll give you so much more
But first, you have to open your heart's door.

It's True

In Your presence there's such peace
All my fears, You release
I may still have some trouble and pain
But with You, more freedom I will gain.
No matter the circumstances, I will trust
To have the victory, it is a must
Your love is overwhelming, it's true
(That thought just made me stop and cry)
'Cause of my sin, You had to die
Ah...read Psalms 34, verse 8
Try the Lord and then just wait
You will see the hand of the Lord move
And His promises, one by one will prove
He loves us more than I can say
You're not alone, get to know Him today.

GOD IS WAITING

When you walk with God, it should be a twenty-four hour walk. God walks with us twenty-four hours a day with no time off, taking no holidays or weekends. The more we praise His name and talk to Him, the more time He spends talking to us. He is in the centre of our praises and loves to hear them. When you think of it, how do you feel when someone tells you they love you? God just wants to love on us all the time, and nothing sounds sweeter than when you hear God's voice say, "I love you."

It always amazes me when God tells me a scripture. God's timing is truly remarkable, and I love when He seems to whisper the scripture to me.

It is true that God knows our every thought, and He can drop a solution on our lap in a wink of an eye.

I mentioned to God the other day how I would like to be a minister or just talk to groups of people, and He heard me. The same day I was doing something in the kitchen and God told me to go for a walk—He had something to show me. Well, I hesitated a little, because this was like exercising, right? But with God all things are possible, and He told me to go again, so I got ready and off I went. Up the lane, I told God I was ready for Him to show me what He was talking about and wouldn't you know it, I heard "Ezekiel 3:9." I walked all around the quarry praying in the Holy Spirit and I kept getting that scripture reference. I went for the Bible as soon as I got home. The verse itself didn't make all that much sense to me, but the explanation below certainly made me sit up and take notice.

3

Verse 9 states, *"I will make your forehead like the hardest stone, harder than flint. Do not be afraid of them or terrified by them, though they are a rebellious people."* The explanation from my Bible (NIV, 1978, 2nd edition) states, "Delivering God's word is a difficult task. The messenger must face hard opposition without fear. The messenger of judgment must personify God's anger against sinful people."

Well, that gives me encouragement to carry on, because I understand by this that God has provisions for me to succeed.

The family next door is also on God's hit list, and guess who has the mission deep in her heart to win them over to the kingdom? If you picked me, you're right. The mom is Aboriginal; she says that church is against her culture, and she will not go there for anything. Her common-law husband is supposed to be Jewish, and there are three children living there also: two teens, a girl and a boy, as well as an eleven-year-old girl. The boy and the eleven-year-old have asked Jesus into their hearts. The boy received Jesus in my living room, and the girl received Jesus while attending Kid's Camp with me. After reading this scripture that God gave me the other night, I felt really bold, so I went next door and asked the neighbours if they wanted to go to breakfast for Good Friday.

My invitation was met by the question, "Why?" "It is Easter and we are neighbours" was my answer. I have been praying that God would knock down the walls around that family: that they would come to church, hear the word and be saved. I encouraged the teenage boy to pray and believe that his mom is going to change, but years of non-Christian thinking and living have taken their toll. Then today, Monday, I sensed in my spirit the scripture, Isaiah 44:2. That was helpful (*"This is what the Lord says—he who made you, who formed you in the womb, and who will help you: do not be afraid, Jacob, my servant, Jeshrun, whom I have chosen"*), and then I sensed Isaiah 45:2-3. *"I will go before you and will level the mountains; I will break down gates of bronze and cut through bars of iron. I will give you hidden treasures stored in secret places, so that you may know that I am the Lord, the God of Israel, who summons you by name. "*

Well, praise God! She was out in front of my home today, giving off negative comments. I tried to make some sense of what she was talking about. My scripture came to me when I started to feel threatened by her remarks. Thank God for the scriptures, which are His promises for us! I got up this morning and decided I was going to fast for breakfast and lunch by only having fruit. I needed to show God that I was serious about this family's salvation.

She knows I am praying for her and she still insists she won't go to church. That is fine, God wants her there, and she will be there!

* * *

Well, after some time away, I started to write again. Things have changed a lot since I started journaling a few years ago. The lady finally moved out, and as much as I tried, she didn't go to church. The others in the family have walked away from God, but God never leaves. He has a way of putting others on the paths of the lost to bring them to the Light.

Get the Blinders Off

Holy Spirit, help the world to see
They are living with blinders on their eyes
So many have to be told
Serving God is better than silver and gold.
Holy Spirit, open their minds
Help them to be forgiving and kind
Their own abilities they cannot trust
Relying on God is a must!
He can help show them the way
And He gives new mercies everyday
Oh, so many are still so lost
They don't realize You paid the cost
I pray Lord, they will turn to You
Then, they'll know how much You love them too!

Renewed Wine Skin

I want to be a new wine skin in Your hand
Fill me up with new wine, help me to understand
Dear Jesus, put me in a tub of oil
So then there's not one squeaky coil
Keep my vision focused, Your face to see
And to bring all others along with me
Turn me inside-out Lord, show Your grace
So being with others, they can see Your face
Thank you for scraping off old residues of life
And applying mercy and eliminating strife
I want to fall in love with You again
Because You first loved me and took away my pain
Take me Lord, stitch me up brand new
So I'll be ready and able to serve only You
Then I'll be ready for a Holy Ghost celebration
As I receive joy by Your great impartation.

Keep Me Strong Please

Oh my Jesus I will follow
Every step along the way
Oh my Jesus I will follow
With the passing of each new day
Keep me on the righteous path
So I'll never know my Creator's wrath
Lift up my arms and keep me strong
So in Your eyes I won't do wrong
May I always be in Your special place
Of total forgiveness and abundant grace.

MY CROWBAR

You might wonder at the title of this chapter, but think about it: how useful is a crowbar, and how many situations can be remedied by the use of one?

Think of the number of situations you have been in that you couldn't get out of or you didn't have a remedy for, but thanks to God, and only through Him, the problem or situation was solved.

I came home from a ladies' coffee break at our church one morning with great expectation about a video called "The Crowbar," by Pastor Buddy Bell.

I got my notebook and pen ready as I made myself comfortable to watch this video. It was not long into the video before I found myself sitting on the floor closer to the TV, as if it would help me get into the same room as this man. The things he was talking about really intrigued me, and I had to stop and start the machine repeatedly in order to write down what he was talking about.

He finally reached the end, explaining a way that God and a crowbar have something in common: how they can both get you out of a certain situation when nothing else will work.

He then asked if we were willing to give it all to God and let Him be our "crowbar," letting Him fix things we cannot possibly do ourselves.

I told God out loud, "I am willing to let You have that place in my life, that You would be the only one and only thing I would rely on."

It is an awesome video, and I would recommend that you watch it. Get ready for change and challenges if you do in fact let God become your "crowbar."

The very same day as I watched this video, I was supposed to play a baseball game with others from work. However, there was also a guest speaker at church, Pastor Yates, and I really wanted to go and hear him.

Now my situation at hand was, should I just go to church and forget about the game? No. Should I call Brenda, the organizer, tell her I would not be going to the game, leave it at that without further specifics, and go to church? That would be the easy way out. Brenda had a way of making your life miserable if you went against her schedule. To be honest, I did wrestle with the different options I had in front of me. But I knew in my heart that I would have to take a stand and tell her I wanted to go to church instead of going to the game. After all, Jesus took a stand for me, and He suffered far more than I would.

I happened to look out the window and said out loud, "God, you could make it rain and I would have my problem solved; I would not have to call her at all."

I laughed and thought, *What are the chances of rain with the sky so blue and the sun so bright*? I made up my mind! I was on my way to the phone to call her when it rang. It was Brenda!

She asked if I had heard the weather report for later on in the day.

I told her, "No, but I was praying for rain," and started to laugh.

Confused, she asked, "What did you say?"

"Oh, nothing, why?"

"I am on my way home with my husband and I still have to stop at the store and I don't think I will have enough time to call the team. They will have to know that the game is going to be postponed. The weather report on the radio just said that we are supposed to get hit with a thunderstorm around 7:00 tonight."

Well, I quickly offered my help calling the rest of the team, which she accepted. I laughed and thanked God for my "crowbar" all the way down the hall to get the team list. I called each one, and after hanging up, proceeded to praise God Almighty. I danced as I sang; I jumped with excitement over how, out of the blue, God was so faithful!

As I was enthusiastically getting ready to go to church, I put a little bit of extra money in my offering envelope. Just when I was about to seal the envelope, I heard, "I told you twenty-five dollars."

Well, with that, I took out the extra money and sealed the envelope.

This proves that God will not ask more of us than what He wants. He asks for ten percent (Numbers 18:25-26). It is so sad to think people smoke, drink, gamble, go to bars and sports games etc., all of which cost money, and they yet don't go to church because all the Church supposedly wants is "your money."

Praise God, while thankfully sitting in the church pew, I just happened to look out the side window at 7:00, and the sun was still shining!

Also that night, God put me in a position of receiving such peace of mind about something that had been interfering with my sleep and duties at work.

When I went to church that night, I first sat half way down from the front and in the middle of the row. I opened my Bible to read something when the voice of God said, "Move up."

I hesitated for a second, closed my Bible, and moved a few rows up. Again, I opened my Bible and started to read.

"Move up" is what I heard, and with that I again hesitated for a second, closed my Bible, and moved up a few more rows.

I had just started to open my Bible when God said, "Move up," and I didn't hesitate this time. I went up to the second row and halfway over.

This time God's voice said, "Move to the first seat."

"Well God, if anyone is watching they're going to think I'm playing musical chairs without the music," I said, but I certainly moved over to the first seat.

Church started, and the music was uplifting and inspiring. Pastor Yates was so interesting to listen to. It was obvious that he was truly a man of God and I was grateful I was sitting there. At different times while speaking, he would pause for a minute or two and I believe that is when God was saying something important to him. He eventually came down from the pulpit and continued to speak. As he was talking and walking back and forth, I could not help but be anxious, feeling like he had something for me. This time, he walked down the aisle a bit, and when he came back past me he stood just off by the front row and looked at me.

"God is going to take away what has been bothering you for months, and it will never bother you again."

I covered my face as I said, "Thank You," and proceeded to cry.

My God, my Crowbar, is so faithful. I was very thankful that I had listened when He told me to move, not really caring what anyone was thinking. I was very thankful I had put only the amount of money He told me to put in the offering envelope. I was extremely thankful for going to that coffee break, hearing about this video, and gong to the office and signing it out.

God has a way of putting us in a position to receive all that He has for us if only we will listen and obey.

My Crowbar

I pray, Dear Jesus, I want it all
Yes, I am willing to pay the price
And when the enemy comes to me to entice
Let me remember, for me, God gave it all.
God gave the miracles I prayed for
He gave me a fresh new start
All I did, was open the door
And let Him come into my heart.
Thank You Dear Jesus for answered prayer
It doesn't matter how big or small
I thank You for Your loving care
And thank God, You gave it Your all.

YOUR MOUTH – FRIEND OR FOE

There is an expression, "You are what you eat."

There is another one I think we should also consider: "You are what you speak."

What you speak over yourself, your family or situation has to be considered carefully. We have to be more aware, and this is a hard habit to get into. How many times do we say things like, "I have a cold and it is never going away," "I will never get a good-paying job," "I am going nowhere fast," "Nobody likes me," "I am going to have a miserable day," or "I am never going to like this new school?"

A friend of mine once told me that her husband was finishing a job and was walking around the house saying, "I'll more than likely get paid only x number of dollars." When he got his payment for the work he had done, sure enough, the amount was exactly what he spoke over himself.

Go big—why not? We serve a big God, and He dreams big and has big plans for us, so why not? As parents, would you rather give your child a little toy car or a special, shining new bike?

I also find it important to ask for God's help with what I put *in* my mouth. Of course, I am not thinking about calories as my hand is pulling the fork away and leaving a fantastic and delicious-tasting bite of cheesecake in my mouth. I am moaning in sheer pleasure as my taste buds dance. It is only later, when I go to put something on that doesn't fit or get on the scales, that I repent and ask for help with discipline. Then I pray that I will remember this frustration when temptation comes again to try my willpower.

James 1:12 says, *"Blessed is the one who perseveres under trial, because having stood the test, that person will receive the crown of life that the Lord has promised to those who love Him."*

Thank God for His Word, because that is where we can go for guidelines. Do you know how many scriptures refer to eating? I was surprised to read them while I went through a weight loss plan through a ladies' group at church a few years ago. It relied on the Bible—how God sees us, not how the scales see us. The program helped most of us ladies a great deal, but like everything else, you have to keep it up or it falls to the side. The Word stays within you, though, and it does help. Here are some of my favourite passages, as well as some that surprised me when I found them. I pray as you read them that they will inspire you and will strengthen you in whatever you are going through. Maybe you will enjoy them simply because they are from God.

- 1 John 4:4 – *"Greater is He that is in you than he that is in the world."*
- Matthew 19:26 – *"But with God all things are possible."*
- Psalm 107:9 – *"He satisfies the thirsty and fills the hungry with good things."*
- Psalm 78:25 – *"Men ate the bread of angels; He sent them all the food they could eat."*
- II Chronicles 15:7 – *"But as for you, be strong and do not give up, for your work will be rewarded."*

These are just a few. It is encouraging to think that God is interested even in this struggle. Even Jesus was tempted, and He is the best example for us to follow.

This subject of the mouth and what we speak can also be applied to our health. We can believe the reports of the doctors or we can believe the Word of the Lord.

There are so many healing verses, tapes and songs about His healing. You need to find a church that teaches and preaches healing. Then, once you get the newfound knowledge that Christ also died on the cross for your sickness and disease, there is no telling what you won't accomplish in the name of Jesus!

God Will Help

Losing weight is for what we strive
So off to the diet store we drive
But wait...
Let God be your diet pill
Instead of yours, it will be His will
Making right choices, He's up for the task
He'll do it but He is waiting for you to ask
He will be with you, He's heard your cry
"O God, how I'd love some of that lemon pie!"
He's right there, He'll guide you through
He will give you wisdom in what to do
God sees your beauty inside and out
With God, you can do it, there is no doubt
When you are tempted but you feel that tug
It'll be God, giving you a hug.

God's Freedom

How can you not feel so humble
When God picks you up when you stumble?
He sent His Son to die on Calvary
He shed His blood for sinners like me,
But as His blood flowed from that tree
Along with it went shame and guilt, He set me free!
No longer in bondage from the past
Thanks to my Heavenly Father, I am free at last.
Then He sent the Holy Spirit so I wouldn't be alone
His guidance and comfort for me He has shown
With God, I no longer have a past
With my Heavenly Father, I'm free at last.
Without a past, Satan can't lie and torment
That's why the hours on the cross were spent
God is truth and Satan is the liar
God took me out of the sin and mire.
Jesus is the one who holds the key
He opened my cell door and set me free
I'm no longer in conflict with the past
Thanks to my Heavenly Father, I'm free at last!

Hebrews Eleven, Verse One

*"Now faith is being sure of what we hope for and
certain of what we do not see."*

Doesn't that verse get you excited?

I remember my friend, Grace, and her husband wanting to have a child naturally, and being told by the doctors that they couldn't because of her medical problems. Grace, being strong in her faith, could not believe that report. She reads her Bible and prays, and just knows God has plans for their lives.

We would talk on the phone and encourage each other with a certain scripture or a praise report about someone, or just talk about the goodness of God. After hanging up the phone, we couldn't help but be on a Holy Spirit high. What a way to start or end a day!

Well the song "Woman with an Issue of Blood" was very precious to us, because the words of the song held the hope we were standing on for Grace. Acts 10:34b states that God does not show favouritism. Whenever we heard that song or we sang it in church, it would lift our spirits up and get us excited all over again.

One afternoon I was listening to Rodney Howard Brown and that song came on. I started to sing to it and just bask in the feeling of the Holy Spirit being right there in my apartment.

When the music was over, I was still feeling His presence; I started to sing unto Him and pray in the Holy Spirit and to tell Jesus how much I loved Him. Well, the tune of "Issue of

Blood" came to me and I started to sing that song out loud, over and over again. Would you believe it: as I was singing, God put new words in my mouth! It amazed me as I heard and sang the words. I had to quickly write them down so I could accurately repeat them to Grace. The first verse was about her and how much she loved God and believed, the second verse about Rick, her husband: "He is a good man, he doesn't know God yet, but hold on—he is going to come." Then there was a verse about Victoria, their young daughter, and how she was a "blessing and a gift," etc. Then the last verse was about "there will be a healthy baby boy." I unfortunately don't have the exact words now, but wow, did that experience ever excite both of us!

Grace and I talked a bit longer then we ended with an agreement that the evening was going to be awesome. I continued to listen to my tape and to sing and praise God. It was like I didn't want to leave His presence: it was just Him and me in my living room. He enjoyed my praises and I enjoyed telling Him how much I loved Him.

In the midst of this, the Holy Spirit told me things about Rick, including how he was going to accept Christ and I would be a part in all of it. I told God to use me in whatever way He wanted—His will was my command.

Again, I heard the voice of God tell me where Grace and I were going to sit in church that night. Earlier that day, I received a phone call about picking up some lady who wanted to come to church but didn't have a ride. I was on such a spiritual high and praising God as I drove to pick up Grace and the other lady. As we drove down the street towards the street light, Grace said, "The Holy Spirit told me to sit in the front row tonight." I started to laugh: to answer the puzzled look on her face, I told her with enthusiasm in my voice, "The Holy Spirit told me to sit in the front row too." While sitting at the light, I was prompted to lay my hand on Grace's stomach and pray, which I did.

We drove around the block four times looking for this woman, thinking that this was a trick of the devil to prevent us from getting the front-row seats. Well, we gave it our best shot and prayed that she got a ride from someone else. Off to church we went, with joy and anticipation, to receive all God had planned for us.

The speaker, Derek Golding, had just flown in from Africa to Toronto and someone picked him up and brought him to our church. He heard about our church through another speaker and made the appropriate arrangements with Pastor Paul. He had a word from God for the church.

We came into the church and up to the front, and wouldn't you know, our two seats were right there for us—the only two left, I might add. After our praise and worship, the message came. "Someone here has been told they have an impossible situation." Now this could have all sorts of implications don't you think? Cancer, heart disease, muscular dystrophy, I mean all sorts of diseases, but then his words became more personal and got right to the heart of the matter! "Someone here has been told they can't have a baby because of their health situation." He was interesting to listen to, and had scriptures to back up everything he was saying. But how did he know to address this exact situation? God gave him a word for our church, and I believe it was for Grace. God sends people your way to let you know things or to confirm things that He has been sharing with you all along. Praise God!!

During his talk he came off the platform, walked across the front of the church, took a few steps down the middle aisle, and then across to the front of the church. Later, when he was on the platform again, he seemed to hesitate as if God was speaking to him at that moment. He excused himself for going with something other than his planned sermon. With that, he came down again—are you ready—to our row, and he prophesied over the whole row. Then he went to a few other people in the row, skipped Grace, and then came to me. He spoke to me as he laid his hands on my shoulders, and down I went on the floor, so I don't know what happened next to anyone.

While on the floor, I could see such brightness, and the voice of God said, "They will have a healthy baby boy and his name will be Daniel." I asked, "Why Daniel; why not Luke or Matthew?" Again God said, "They will have a healthy baby boy and call him Daniel." Eventually I got up and sat back down, and Derek Golding was already preaching again. Near the end he had us all stand up and said, "Someone here has been told they can't have a baby—who is it?" Grace and I just held each other's hand at our side and then he looked at Grace and said, "Is it you?" He asked her to come forward. He laid hands on her and spoke over her and she went down under the power of the Holy Spirit. I had taken a few steps toward her and I had my hands out, praying in the Holy Spirit quietly as if she was my own sister. He looked at me and said, "You have the joy; lay hands on her stomach." I quickly went to her, knelt down, laid my hand on her and began to pray. Within a few seconds she received holy laughter. Wow, what a rush! I started to laugh. When she sat up, we hugged each other and I whispered in her ear that God told me they were going to have a healthy baby boy called Daniel. She chuckled and said, "Rick's middle name is Daniel."

Is God an awesome God? He is so faithful, patient, understanding, and rewarding.

If nothing else ever happened to me, that would have been enough to keep my faith level high, but God had more doors opening for us that night. He was telling me things to share with Rick when I dropped Grace home, and of course he was open to hearing all that I had to say. Victoria couldn't sleep, so we all went for a drive—would you believe, all the way to London? Of course, the conversation all the way was about my Lord and Saviour and what he could do for Rick. Possibilities kept coming to my mind. He was open and talked with respect and interest. On the way home we talked a bit more. Then it seemed like the time to be quiet and let him digest what he had heard and for Grace and me to quietly pray. We plant the seed and the Holy Spirit waters and nurtures it. It was less than a month after that night that the Holy Spirit brought me to their house again. Even though Rick was busy cleaning the aquarium, he was interested enough to ask key questions about God and he was open for the answers. I kept encouraging him by speaking into his life all that I believed God had planned for him.

It was now time for a smoke break, so outside we went to continue on with this life-changing conversation. Outside, without prompting, with a cigarette in his hand, he asked Jesus into his heart. God let me be there to witness that; He gave me a gift because I was obedient to His voice.

This was His prophetic word coming to pass!

* * *

I remember the first time I was a greeter at the door at church, which was Grace's first time being there. She prayed that there would be someone in the church who would take her under their wing. I immediately felt that she should sit with me rather than sit alone, and we have been like sisters since then.

Grace and her husband invited me over for coffee one night. We went outside on the front step for some fresh air, and out of the blue, Rick said, "I want to ask you a question and I want you to answer off the top of your head: why do you think you came into our lives?"

I answered without a blink of an eye, "So I can have a sister's relationship with Grace because I can't have this kind of relationship with my own sisters, and as for you, God is going to allow me to see you become a Christian. Victoria is a joy to watch and I could never have kids, so this way I can experience things I missed." I think my explanation kind of took him aback, but he told me it was a good one.

Why did I share all this with you? It is so important that we keep a high level of faith, so high the devil can't affect us when he tries to knock us down. God is faithful to His word, and there are so many scriptures to encourage us and to show us the way. We have to submit to God, obey His word and serve Him and only Him, and then we get to receive all the treasures, the blessings, the answers to prayer, and best of all, His presence, when we go through life's storms.

Going through this challenge together with Grace taught me a lot about dealing with "impossible situations." If you find yourself in similar circumstances, read, confess out loud, and meditate on the following scriptures 3 times a day for a week.

- Mark 5:25-34 – the lady with an issue of blood
- Matthew 17:20 – faith the size of a mustard seed
- Mark 11:22-23 – tell that mountain to go into the sea
- Proverbs 18:21 – *"The tongue has the power of life and death, and those who love it will eat its fruit."*

There are so many things the Holy Spirit revealed to Grace and me. One of us would receive a confirmation through a scripture that was given, or a word in conversation with somebody that seemed to have nothing to do with the situation. I would like to share some examples; after reading them, I am sure that you, too, will feel like Grace and I did.

Visions of Babies

I called Grace one afternoon. We could only talk for a minute, since she was waiting for a phone call, so I hung up the phone and proceeded to do my jazzercise for the day. I was on the floor doing those great sit-ups when it started happening. Each time I sat up I would get this vision—Grace, Rick, the pastor, their baby and myself. It was a Baby Dedication.

I must say, those sit-ups became unnaturally fast as a result! RRRIIIINNNNNGGGG—what a time for an interruption! I answered the phone and it was Grace. I couldn't get my vision out of my mouth before Grace was bubbling to tell me of hers.

When we had hung up earlier, she was doing her dishes while I was exercising. As she washed, she started to get a vision about Rick, herself, the pastor, their baby and me. It was a Baby Dedication. She was just getting ready to give God the glory and praise for this miracle when her phone call came in. I just about jumped through the phone!

Terry E.

"God is no respecter of persons," as Terry E. knows very well.

He was young, married and planning a family of his own. He was busy working in a church with the young people; he had a plan, and he was in control. Then one day, during a routine checkup, the doctors found something off-balance with his blood test results. It is probably a virus. A few weeks passed with no change to the blood test results. Suddenly, out of nowhere, he finds himself at the hospital awaiting the results from a bone marrow aspiration they have just performed on his body. The next hour seems like an eternity. The doctor appears and asks him to have a seat in a private room. He looks Terry in the eye and tells him he has leukemia.

That was nine years ago, and by the grace of God, he is alive and well with a beautiful family.

Satan strikes when things are going well: when our guard is down, when we are comfortable. In John 10:10, Jesus says, *"The thief comes only to steal and kill and destroy; I have come that they may have life, and have it to the full."*

Through the teaching Terry had received prior to this time, he knew that God still heals people today. One of His names is Jehovah Rapha, our Healer. Terry knew that His Word contains a specific promise for his situation, as it does for all of our needs. The day he was diagnosed was Good Friday, the day that Jesus died on the cross for our sins and sicknesses. Isaiah 53:5 states, *"But he was pierced for our transgressions, he was crushed for our iniquities; the punishment that brought us peace was upon him, and by his wounds we are healed."*

The next day, Terry stole away for a time of prayer and fasting, determined to receive a word from God he could cling to. After a time of purifying his heart and life through prayer, the word came. God led him to two verses. The first was Psalm 32:8, which says, *"I will instruct you and teach you in the way you should go; I will counsel you with my loving eye on you."* He knew God was by his side. The second scripture was Proverbs 3:7-8, stating, *"Do not be wise in your own eyes; fear the Lord and shun evil. This will bring health to your body and nourishment to your bones."* Leukemia is a cancer of the blood, and blood cells originate from the bone marrow. He had his specific promise from God.

Over that weekend much prayer had taken place, as the Word of God advises. By the time he was admitted into the hospital, God had blessed him with a special gift of faith. He knew in his heart he was healed. Hebrews 11:1 says, *"Now faith is being sure of what we hope for and certain of what we do not see."*

On Easter Monday, the day Jesus rose from the dead victorious over hell, death and the grave, Terry was admitted into the hospital. He called his boss from his hospital room to tell him he would not be coming to work. First thing Tuesday morning, they began chemotherapy.

He spent the next eight-and-a-half weeks in the hospital undergoing, and recovering from, chemotherapy. During that period he experienced a total fall of the physical man, and yet he experienced such closeness to Jesus, who enables us to walk through trials, tribulations and temptations. 1 Corinthians 10:13 states, *"No temptation has seized you except what is common to man. And God is faithful; he will not let you be tempted beyond what you can bear. But when you are tempted, he will also provide a way out so that you can stand up under it."* It is amazing what an individual can walk through with Jesus at their side.

God rewards us for our faith and overcoming. Today, Terry stands as a whole man in spirit, soul and body. After the chemotherapy, he was advised that he would not be able to have children, but the Word says in Psalm 128 that those who fear the Lord will be fruitful and blessed with children. Terry now has two beautiful children.

Revelation 12:11 says, *"They triumphed over [Satan] by the blood of the Lamb and by the word of their testimony."* Terry testifies that Jesus is the same yesterday, today and forever, and that He is able to heal you just as He healed him.

God is no respecter of persons. Hell, death and the grave have been denied!!

Karen W's Testimony

This is a testimony of a woman who is currently married and has three children. In the early 1960s, she and Ted appeared to have a typical marriage. What the world didn't know was that Karen was feeling very frustrated and tied down. She was always with the children, with very little emotional support from her husband since he spent a lot of time at the race car tracks.

Karen didn't have anywhere to turn for help except for her doctor. She started to take prescription drugs to get relief, comfort and some sort of release. Over time, Karen became a prescription drug addict. Ted didn't notice, of course, since he was seldom at home. Unfortunately, there came a time when the drugs were not helping anymore.

I trust Karen's story will touch you and give you hope. The following is written in her words.

* * *

January 28, 1965, was the turning point for our marriage. We had been asked to go to a church service, and we reluctantly went. We just didn't have anything better to do but church! We talked about it, and with some hesitation decided to go. That night we asked Jesus into our hearts before it was time to leave for home. No more drugs. Christ was the answer!

In 1973 I was baptized in the Holy Spirit. I was truly enjoying my relationship with Christ and learning more about Him and His unconditional love for me. At this time, Ted and I also had another child, a son, and things were so much better at home. We both saw things much differently and experienced the difference God was making in our marriage and family.

I started feeling sick and because of the severity, I did not put off going to the doctors. On January 13, 1978, I was to have an operation on the pancreas.

The next day my husband and I were told the unthinkable: I had lymphoma cancer.

Here I was, a born-again Christian wife and mother, reading my Bible, going to church and doing all the things I should be doing, and now I was diagnosed with cancer.

Remember, just because a person is a Christian does not mean that only good things will happen to them. The difference is Christ and how we go through the tragedies of life compared to how we handle the same situation without Christ. One main difference is that you are not alone; Jesus never leaves us nor forsakes us. Press into Jesus when you go through sickness or rough times; stay in prayer; focus on Jesus and not on the situation. I can say this because I have personally experienced when Jesus pulled me through and I had victory.

While I spent hours in the hospital bed, I would pray and read my Bible. I would ask God to give me a scripture to stand on no matter what the doctors had to say. Psalm 50:15 is what God gave me: *"...and call upon me in the day of trouble; I will deliver you, and you will honour me."*

I had three teenagers checking out healing scriptures, plus a four year old son. Psalm 107:20 states, *"He sent out his word and healed them; he rescued them from the grave."* Matthew, Mark, Luke and John were encouraging gospels for me. I believed the scriptures, not the situation. 1 Peter 2:24 and Psalm 103:3 talk about God healing all diseases. Matthew 8:17 says, *"He Himself took our infirmities and bore our sickness"* (NKJV). I took these words on faith, claiming the healing scriptures for my situation.

Ted brought in a cassette player and healing tapes for me to listen to. No one was allowed around me who did not believe in my healing. This is so important for all of us: don't have negative people around you.

I could not take the full treatment of radiation because I was so sensitive to it. I was all of sixty-five pounds by now.

I lifted my arms to God and I told Him, "I know I don't look healed. The Word says in 1 Peter 2:24; '...*who Himself bore our sins in His own body on the tree, that we, having died to sins, might live for righteousness—by whose stripes you were healed*'" (NKJV).

After quoting the Word, I started to feel the power of God come upon me—on my hand and down my arm and through my body. I knew right then that God had healed me.

When Ted came into visit me, he couldn't see the healing that I was so convinced I had received. I told Ted about the awesome experience I'd had with God, and how I felt that healing power come over me. Ted was only going by what he could see on the outside—the outward condition.

Eventually I was able to go to church and I was asked to share with the congregation how I was feeling.

"I don't look or feel healed, but the Word says I am healed." As I confessed what the Word says, I felt strength rise up within me.

It didn't happen overnight. It took two years to reach my original weight of 127 pounds.

1 Timothy 6:12 refers to God giving us strength to fight the good fight of faith.

My family fought it along with me. Each one originally had their own response to the news of cancer. Ted even wanted to go to the lawyer and make sure everything was up-to-date. His lawyer, along with the doctor, suggested he should go pick out a coffin and make funeral arrangements.

When I would leave the hospital and come home on weekends, there would be times that I would be sick, and our four-year-old son would lay hands on me and pray. He was not told that his mommy had cancer; he just knew his mommy was sick.

The one who is sick needs support, not pity.

I prayed, thanked God, quoted His Word, and rebuked the enemy that had caused the sickness in Jesus' name. I commanded the cause of my sickness to leave and every symptom to be destroyed by the power of my Lord who is present now. Then I thanked Him for answering. When we thank God, it is showing in faith that we believe He has answered our prayers.

Twenty-five years later I am still going strong serving Jesus.

Hebrews 10:23 says, *"Let us hold fast the confession of our hope without wavering, for He who promised is faithful"* (NKJV).

I trust this has helped you in what you may be going through or just to have knowledge. The Word says, *"My people are destroyed for lack of knowledge"* (Hosea 4:6, NKJV).

* * *

If you don't know Christ, you don't know what you would do in the situation Karen was in. Ask Christ now! It is so easy; just say this to Him: "Jesus, come into my heart and cleanse me. I believe that You died for me and You rose again. I now confess that You are my Lord and Saviour and I choose to serve only You. Amen." Congratulations! You are now a child of God.

The next step is to be empowered by the Holy Spirit. It is a gift from God, and He wants everyone to have it. When you pray for the Baptism of the Holy Spirit, ask God to give you the Holy Spirit; tell Him, "I receive your gift now, in Jesus' name."

The Book of Acts talks about this. Acts 1:5 says that *"... you shall be baptized with the Holy Spirit"* (NKJV). Acts 1:8 follows: *"But you shall receive power when the Holy Spirit has come upon you;*

and you shall be witnesses to Me in Jerusalem, and in all Judea and Samaria, and to the end of the earth" (NKJV).

Hebrews 11:6 tells us further, *"And without faith it is impossible to please God, because anyone who comes to him must believe that he exists and that he rewards those who earnestly seek him."*

He loves us and wants to bless us beyond any imagination we may possess. If you, as a parent, want to give good gifts to your children, think of how much more God wants to give to you!

James 1:17 states, *"Every good gift and perfect gift is from above, coming down from the Father of the heavenly lights, who does not change like shifting shadows."*

Don't stay gazing at your circumstances; think of the One who took all of that to the cross.

When Karen stood on God's promises and said them back to Him, it caused Him to act. Romans 2:11 says, *"For God does not show favouritism."*

What personally did it for me was wondering if it was in God's will to heal. The answer was found in Mark 1:40-41. *"A man with leprosy came to [Jesus] and begged him on his knees, 'If you are willing, you can make me clean.' Filled with compassion, Jesus reached out his hand and touched the man. "I am willing,"* he said. *'Be clean!'"*

For some reason, that really came off the page the day I was reading and doing my paper on "Jesus the Healer." This lesson was taken as part of a home course from Faith College in Saskatoon, Saskatchewan. It is an excellent course and really helped me understand a lot more about the Bible, the Church, and the pastor, to mention only a few things. It is well worth looking into.

Jesus the Healer

Thank you Jesus for how the Word would show
In 1 Cor. 4:11, "Buffet" means blow after blow
I know by the Word I can always stand
And tell the devil to go, with a Jesus command.
It was Satan who put a thorn in Paul's side
And it was God who changed him on his donkey
   ride.
The devil likes to confuse, says John 8:44
So be careful what you think, don't open that door.
In 2 Cor. 12:9, God did not say "No"
But His power and ability on our behalf did show
Humble ourselves and God will exalt us
Sometimes how I live I wonder why He would fuss
Now to save yourself from getting into a tiff
When you pray to God, don't use the word "If"
Healing and divine health are always God's will
Use this as your prescription instead of a pill.
Our assurance is written in Proverbs 4:22
Not just for some, but all of us, me and you.
What did it for me, was the leper in Mark 1:40, 41
How Jesus is definitely the Willing One!
He is no respecter of persons, Acts 10:34
And He can do it again just like He did it before.

He is in Control

God never promised you a rose garden
But peace and joy so your heart wouldn't harden
When you suffer do not be afraid
He's your shield when Satan tries to invade
God can help you suffer well
I've been there, I can tell
Satan attacks your heart and soul
But let God take control
He will be with you through the pain
Trust in Him and the victory you'll gain
Try to think of it as a Godly test
Have faith that God will do the rest.

PSALM THIRTY-FOUR

When I was just a baby Christian, Geri Ross gave me a One Year Bible. Each day I would faithfully read God's Word. As I would be reading, I would sometimes think about a scripture I'd heard someone quote and think that it was neat when I found it.

At different times I would ask God, "When will I get 'my' scripture verse, like these other people have?" One evening I was reading and it happened. The scripture for that day was Psalm 34, verses one to ten. As I was reading, I could see my early experiences at Eastdale Christian Outreach Centre reflected.

I would like to go through those verses and explain what I am referring to.

Verses 1-3 say *"I will praise the Lord no matter what happens. I will constantly speak of His glories and grace. I will boast of all His kindness to me. Let all who are discouraged take heart. Let us praise the Lord together and exalt His name"* (TLB). This seemed like what I was doing at Eastdale. I felt great talking and thinking about all the good things God had been doing for me in what seemed like such a short time. No matter what, I knew God was with me. We have an excellent praise and worship time at Eastdale. Do you know God loves to hear our praise and worship? What happens when we praise the Lord? We praise God for His power, because He uses that power in love to give His people victory. This is an explanation for the verse I have in my Bible. One time, during praise and worship, I could see what I thought was God sitting on His throne enjoying our singing. I could see His sleeve moving to the music as it rested on the armchair.

When we stopped singing I distinctly heard God say, "Oh, don't stop yet!"

The Holy Spirit must have said something, because after a couple of minutes of spiritual silence, we started to sing the chorus of the last song again. I could sense that God was pleased.

Verse 4 states, *"For I cried to Him and He answered me! He freed me from all my fears"* (TLB). I did cry out to Him about different things, and He answered my cries. One example: when I had to do the weekly paperwork at work, for some reason it never went smoothly for me. I asked God to be with me—that all of my inventory would balance and the totals for the bank would be right the first time. He answered in so many ways, opening my eyes to items I missed; I had no fear of things going wrong. I was out of there that night on time and it all worked out well. Praise God!

Verse 5 says, *"Others too were radiant at what He did for them. Theirs was no downcast look of rejection!"* (TLB). I remember sitting in Church thinking how these singers looked so alive, and marvelling at the peace that was all over their faces as they sang about God and how much He loved us. One singer, Barb Engel, stands out in my mind. When she was singing, you would get the feeling she was singing in front of Jesus all by herself.

Verse 6 continues, *"This poor man cried to the Lord—and the Lord heard him and saved him out of his troubles"* (TLB). I remember the pastor asking anyone who needed prayer to come forward. One man came up right away, looking like he had the world on his shoulders. I had only been going there for a short time, but I had such an urge to go over and put my hand on his shoulder and tell him I was standing with him and that he wasn't alone. I found out that his name was Ted, and his wife had just gone through a double bypass.

Verse 7 states, *"For the Angel of the Lord guards and rescues all who reverence Him"* (TLB). Well, it sure makes me feel good to know that His words say that He is providing me with protection.

Verse 8 tells us, *"Oh, put God to the test and see how kind He is! See for yourself the way His mercies shower down on all who trust in Him"* (TLB). What excitement that stirs up in me! How about you? I have seen and experienced how kind God is—and just think, it is not a temporary thing; it happens all the time as I fellowship with my God.

Verse 9 says, *"If you belong to the Lord, reverence Him; for everyone who does this has everything he needs"* (TLB). Now, His word says I will lack for nothing; He is all I need. I had really never heard or thought of that before—what a revelation!

Finally, Verse 10 states, *"Even strong young lions sometimes go hungry, but those of us who reverence the Lord will never lack any good thing"* (TLB). See, I don't have to be someone with power, fancy clothes and cars, or to be a "big shot," for God to love me. I am His now, and He wants to look after me.

Well, after reading this I started to cry, as I realized what it was going to be like serving God. I put my opened Bible to my chest and cried like a baby, because I knew those were the scriptures God had planned for me. These scriptures were so close to my heart. I realized something then: a scripture is yours when it ministers to you personally. Someone else could read that psalm and get something totally different from me, because they didn't have those experiences.

I remember one time when I was going to sing at the Wesleyan Church in Brockville, my hometown. The night before, I received a scripture while I was sleeping. It gave me encouragement for the task at hand. It also provided an opportunity for me to witness to the congregation that morning as to how God will always supply the support we need to do His work.

When we are obedient, He is there for us! When we are not obedient, He is still there waiting for us to realize how much we need Him.

This promise is found in Proverbs 16:20, *"Whoever gives heed to instruction prospers, and blessed is he who trusts in the Lord."* How could I fail when a scripture like that was given to me?

This Place of Grace

God's grace is where I stand
The Holy Spirit will help me to understand
I stand in a place of God's total supply
On faith and God I completely rely
I am in this place that He calls Grace
And Satan doesn't want me in the open space
Where God looks down and totally blesses
He wants me to live without the stresses.
Christ has come that we can truly be free
So don't be burdened by the yoke of slavery
I stand amazed at God's eternal love
And He showers me with blessings from above
Lord, may I always be able to stand in this place
Of Your total supply and Your abundant grace.

Encouraged

It is encouraging to know
When I die, where I will go
Regardless...
I am encouraged as I walk with You
Relying on the Word to show me what to do
I am encouraged by all I see
All Your beauty that surrounds me
You gave me family so I'm not alone
Made me unique, I'm not a clone
So it's not just the hope of heaven for me
It is really knowing that You died for me
This hope I have is an anchor for my soul
Holy Spirit, help me, so that I may reach my goal.

My Friend, the Holy Spirit

I have experienced such an awesome relationship with the Holy Spirit. He talks to me, shows me things, comforts me, and reminds me how special I am to Jesus. He is always there, even when I am feeling alone or feeling like I am a failure. He knows exactly what is on the Father's heart, and He reveals that to me. John 14:26 says, *"But the Counselor, the Holy Spirit, whom the Father will send in my name, will teach you all things and remind you of everything I have said to you."* Of course, if I don't talk to Him, how can He feel like He can talk to me? This is the same as in any relationship.

Jesus told us that God was going to send us a Comforter. When you read John 15:26, it also confirms that God sent Him: *"When the Advocate comes, whom I will send to you from the Father— the Spirit of truth who goes out from the Father—he will testify about me."* In the side notes to my NIV Bible (1978, 2nd edition), the following is written:

The Holy Spirit – Teaches; the Spirit of truth guides disciples into all truth. He reveals God's truth even more fully than Jesus Himself had been able to do, because Jesus did His teaching before the cross. The Spirit does His teaching after the cross and the resurrection, which is the fullest self-revelation of God. Jesus sometimes spoke in figurative language. After the resurrection, the truth could be expressed in clear language. The Spirit reveals the meaning of the cross and resurrection, and brings glory to Christ.

In this chapter, I pray that the experiences that I share with you will cause you to be hungry for the Holy Spirit and will lift up your faith to a new level. It is so exciting to see what

God has planned for me when I hear that special voice and obey. He also has plans for you!

Monique

I was just getting ready to leave work one day when one of the part-time girls came in for her shift. This girl was young, pretty, and always smiling—except for today. Instead of her bright blue eyes, I saw only sadness and redness. I gave her a few minutes to herself in the washroom before going in to see if I could help, even if just to listen.

She told me the problem: the doctor had given her some bad news, and she would need surgery for the tumour found in her head. Doubly painful was the fact that a friend of hers had had the same operation two years ago in Poland, and she hadn't made it.

I held her, as her warm tears soaked my sweater. I told her that only God could help, and I was going to be praying for her.

I assured her that God had better and bigger plans for her than some old surgery. She seemed to get herself together and ready for her shift. I prayed for her on the way home.

While standing in my living room praising God, praying in the Holy Spirit, the Holy Spirit started to reveal something to me. I wasn't sure at first, but as I kept praying, it became clearer. I saw a ball of some sort, and eventually it started to look like a brain. It had a small round thing in a certain spot, and as I was praying and getting excited, I saw it getting smaller and smaller! When I finally calmed down, I began to praise and thank God for the awesome time I'd had with Him.

I phoned work and told Monique to call me as soon as she got home. The phone rang at 9:30, and it was her. I reminded her of my promise to pray for her and then began to tell her what the Holy Spirit had shown me. I suggested that she call her doctor the next day and arrange to have those tests done again, before she went under the knife. She assured me that she would do that.

With her working part-time and some changes in work responsibilities, I didn't see her for a bit after that. When I did, she told me that the doctor had agreed to do the tests again. She then told me something that only God could have arranged.

Monique had a big smile on her face and a familiar twinkle in her eye.

"Oh Brenda, I was at the doctor's office the other day and the results were different," she said. "The doctor said that the tests showed the tumour getting smaller and smaller, and he believes it will dissolve on its own!"

Hooray, no surgery! Isn't God a great God?

Wayne's Lump

I started working at a new job and couldn't help but notice that one of my supervisors, Wayne, had a lump in the middle of his back the size of a golf ball. I could see it through his shirt, and I wondered what it was.

God heard me! One morning, I was minding my own business, just getting out of the shower, when the Holy Spirit told me to let Wayne know that God was going to heal that lump. I needlessly reminded the Holy Spirit that I had been working only a few months at this new job. To tell my supervisor that God was going to heal him...well, I just didn't know if I should.

God convinced me that He would be with me all the way. After all, would my own father tell me to tell someone something if it would only make me look ridiculous? No, he wouldn't, and neither would my Heavenly Father.

Well, when I got the sign I had asked for, which was time alone with Wayne, I decided that I would say something. I mentioned to him that I couldn't help but notice his back, and then I inquired about the lump.

He told me some of the history of it and how it had started. I then told him what had happened to me that morning before leaving for work. He was sceptical, but as he walked away he said, "You keep praying, Brenda."

I did keep praying, because I knew the Holy Spirit wouldn't show me this without a plan to see it to completion. The Bible states, *"He Himself bore our sins in his body on the tree, so that we might die to sins and live in righteousness: by his wounds you have been healed"* (1 Peter 2:24).

As weeks went by, I continued praying and believing—and when I had the opportunity to ask Wayne for an update, I would ask with anticipation.

I can't remember exactly how much time had passed from our initial conversation until the final one, when I asked Wayne what had happened to the lump—well, the lump was no more. It seems that he woke up during the night with a hot, wet sensation on his back. He woke his wife to see what was happening, and she told him that all of the infection and whatever else was causing this lump was draining out of it. After his wife had cleaned it all up, all that was needed was a bandage!

The funny thing was, the doctor had been scheduled to take the lump out at one point, but on the day of the appointment he had to cancel because of an emergency. I told him that I believed that happened because God had been planning to heal him, not the doctor.

He is still sceptical, but I know in my heart that God did what He said He would do. Praise the Lord! He used me to show that He is faithful, and just maybe plant a seed in Wayne.

Rudy's Mom

I was involved with a home group from church. One night, before the meeting started, I mentioned what God was doing with me and the preceding two medical situations that the Holy Spirit had revealed to me.

One of the gentlemen asked me if I had to know the person before I could see anything.

I told him I didn't know—what God had been doing was all new to me—and asked him why.

He informed us that his mom had been suffering with terrible headaches and had been under the care of her doctor for quite some time. It seemed that the doctors could not figure out why, even after many tests.

Well, the meeting started, and everyone was silent as we listened to the leader. I must admit, I did ask God out of curiosity why his mom had the headaches. I thought of a few potential causes but received no confirmations. It is funny now that I think of it, but when I asked God, it was like I expected Him to answer me right there. The Holy Spirit started to show me this little bone at the top of her spine at the base of her skull; it looked like a little square box. Once I got that vision I couldn't sit still! I wanted to jump up and praise God, but the Holy Spirit is a gentleman; that would only bring attention to me and interrupt the meeting. I patiently waited as the teaching ended and the prayer time started. I was the third person to pray.

I thanked God for showing me the bone and asked Him to please show the doctors what He had shown me. Over coffee and cookies there was a barrage of questions from the son, but I could only tell him what I had seen. Apparently while praying I was squeezing his hand, and he complimented me on my strong grip.

By the time I got home and ready for bed, it was quite late. As my head hit the pillow, I saw that little box again, only this time there were jagged lines leaving it in all directions. It reminded me of a cartoon image of a crash or lightning. Can you picture it now in your mind? The next afternoon, the man's wife called me to tell me that she had heard from her mother-in-law. She went on, with a sweet sound of thankfulness in her voice, to tell me that her mother-in-law had gone to her doctor's appointment that morning. The doctor got "the idea to do an X-ray" and the results showed a hairline fracture in the bone that God had showed me the night before.

As soon as the doctor told her that, she immediately replied, "That's right, I had a car accident about four years ago." Isn't my God great?

A Businessman

Sometimes you want to go to bed with a light, interesting book, but you're not sure just which one to take. That was how this evening started.

Again, quite simply and innocently, I had one book in my hand, yet it didn't feel right. Then the Holy Spirit brought my attention to another one called *Lord Teach Me to Pray*, by Kay Arthur. I opened it and found out that it is a 28-day study on how to pray. I completed the first day of the study and did the homework, which was to write a prayer out. I must admit, asking the Holy Spirit to help me was sure beneficial. My initial prayer was flat and boring, but when my Friend helped me, it was different! Well, I still wasn't sleepy, so I went on with day two, and after doing the homework for that day, I put the book down and turned off the light.

I think I had been asleep for about an hour and a half when the phone woke me up with an apology on the other end. It was my friend Cathy, telling me that although she had thought it was too late, her husband, Rudy, had told her to call me and ask me to pray.

They'd just had a phone call from very dear friends who were cutting a Christian album. The money that was promised to them didn't come in. They had the rent of the studio and the band to pay, and all that goes along with an endeavour like that.

I laughed and told her that she was not going to believe what just happened to me. I proceeded to tell her about how God had brought it to my attention to read this particular book tonight. I assured her that I would pray, and I hung up and got on my knees and started. It didn't take me more than a couple of seconds to realize that when the Holy Spirit was praying with me, I didn't sound like I used to. I got the prayer out, prayed it again, and then put in the request for these people who needed a financial miracle. Glory to God, I bet it wasn't more than two minutes of praying before I heard the voice of God!

As I knelt in my dark bedroom, I was amazed to hear God say, "I have everything under control. A businessman is going to help the Neilsons out."

I looked up and asked, "God, is that You?"

Again I heard, "I have everything under control. A businessman in going to help the Neilsons out." Well, I got up and phoned Cathy back.

With enormous confidence in my voice I said, "I just heard from God and He said that He has everything under control; a businessman is going to help the Neilsons out. As far as I am concerned, it is a done deal."

Cathy laughed and said, "Well, then, it is a done deal!" We spoke a bit more, just some small talk, and then hung up.

Two days later, I received a phone call. It was Cathy; first she asked me if I was sitting down. I told her "yes" and then she proceeded. She'd heard from Neilsons; apparently they were taking a break from singing when this man, a total stranger, came over to the leader.

He introduced himself and then said, "I don't quite understand, but it has been put on my heart to help you people out financially; how much do I make out this cheque for? By the way, here is my business card with my phone numbers; call me whenever I can help you again." His business is in Winnipeg, Manitoba, while the recording studio is in Ontario.

Well, when I hung up the phone, I praised my God with such excitement and joy. I danced, I jumped, and I sang unto Him. Again, He is faithful and I had been used by Him.

God wants to use us as we die unto the self and let Jesus live. He is always looking for willing vessels to do His work for the kingdom of God.

April 25

My friend Grace and I were talking on the phone on a Monday night and she was telling me about being in church the previous evening. During the service she started to hear, out of nowhere, a certain date. She didn't know if it was the devil trying to break her concentration or if it was actually God speaking to her. She was hoping it was God and asked, it was Him, that He would have someone else come up to her and confirm the date before she went home.

Well, people talked to her after out in the vestibule but nobody said that date. I mentioned a few on the phone and she said no to all of them, so I gave up. She didn't even tell the date to her husband, so that if someone did say it, she would know it had come from God rather than Rick having let it slip when talking to someone. We talked a bit longer and hung up, feeling like we were on a spiritual high.

I got on my knees and prayed. "God, please tell someone that date and let them be talking to Grace and have them mention it to her. She would be so happy and relieved to know that it was Your voice she heard Sunday night. While I have Your attention, Lord, would You use me? You know how much I love her, so would you please tell me the date?"

At bedtime, I took the dog out for his usual thing and I was admiring how beautiful the sky looked and telling God how great He was. Before I went in the house, I could see "APRIL 25" printed on my forehead in big black letters. I don't know if it was because I wasn't expecting an answer so fast or if I had something else on my mind or because it was too late to call her, but I left it at that. *Well, if this comes to me again then I'll know it is God*, I thought to myself.

I was at work the next day when I saw "APRIL 25" again. I asked, "God, is that You?" Would you believe it, I heard back, "Ask Grace what the significance of April 25th is."

While at work, a woman came over to my workplace and asked if I would pray for one of the worker's babies, who had just been transferred to the London hospital in serious condition. I told her I would.

I walked into my apartment and phoned Grace to tell her about this baby and to ask her to pray also. We talked, and then I told her that I had tried to reach her in the morning to inquire about April 25th.

She yelled, "That's the date I heard in church on Sunday."

I told her I heard His voice say, "Ask Grace what the significance of April 25th is." Well we had goose bumps and joy and we laughed. As I sat on my couch later, I sat with such amazement and humbleness, to think that in so small a thing, God had actually heard and answered me.

The Lost Keys

One morning I had a specialist appointment in London, about 50 miles from Woodstock. I couldn't find my keys anywhere. I looked in, over, and under everything, and still came up empty-handed. I started to get a bit upset, and then I remembered the Bible lesson that I was taking from Faith College in Saskatchewan. The lesson is called "Prayer, the Absolute Solution." Well, praise God, my Friend the Holy Spirit brought Psalm 34:17 to my attention: *"The righteous cry out, and the Lord hears them; He delivers them from all their troubles."* I thank God that His word does not return empty (Isaiah 55:11b).

Well, I went to my appointment, after getting a spare key from the landlord. Fortunately, I had an extra car key. I was singing praises to God on my trip and thinking about how great He was, how much He must love me, and how much I love Him. I knew that before the day was out, He would show me where my keys were.

Coming up the elevator to my apartment, I chuckled to myself and said, "Okay Holy Spirit, the hide and seek game is over; where are my keys?"

I got a vision of the lazy boy recliner in the living room, and saw my keys between the seat and the arm. Well, I was so settled in my mind with that vision, I put the dog out and then thought, *Oh yeah, those keys!* Sure enough, they were exactly where My Friend had showed me they would be. I'd looked there that morning, but I guess I didn't put my hand down far enough. The amazing thing is, they were on the exact side of the chair that I saw in my vision.

Actually, I am thankful that I didn't find them on my own that morning. I spent the whole day talking, singing and resting in peace. I knew that God was enjoying this time together, as I was. Also, now I have a testimony of God's goodness, and proof that God hears and answers!

So many times, I truly experience Him answering me when I ask for help to find things. The Holy Spirit is amazing, and I appreciate Him so much. He definitely guides our every step, if we allow Him to.

Holy Spirit – My Friend

How does the Holy Spirit come from within?
O my goodness, where do I begin?
Call, then wait upon His Holy name
When He comes, you'll never be the same.
Sometimes I have covered my face and cried
Other times laughed and went along for the ride.
He can make you laugh from down in your belly
You can't help but feel like a bowl full of jelly.
He brings out things from the past
After you feel, "I'm free at last!"
You may act funny but you don't care
Oh search Him out, if you dare...
The feeling is rather hard to express
But it sure is awesome, I will confess.
The Holy Spirit is your Friend
Every day, from beginning to end,
When you feel Him upon you, go with the flow
Submit to Him fully and away you go!
Be careful, the devil tries and tries
To steal Him before your very eyes.
At the beginning of each new day
For your sake, take time to pray.
Sent from God, a Comforter to be
Just listen to Him and you will see
Your life will be changed, and for the good
As you let Him lead and do as you should.

PRAYING IN THE HOLY SPIRIT

When we don't know how to pray, the Holy Spirit can show us. I have seen and heard many things while praying in the Holy Spirit. It is rewarding in several ways, but one benefit is receiving clarity when praying about something that needs to be dealt with.

I remember one time when a prayer request came to the prayer team's attention, a "for your eyes only" sort of thing, at least for the time being. I was at home when I got the request, and proceeded to pray. I honestly didn't know how to pray for the situation, but God did. As I proceeded to pray in the spirit, God started to reveal things to me, and the more I pressed in, the more He would reveal. I stayed on my knees in prayer until I felt as if things had been accomplished. I phoned and left a message for the people who were directly involved. I told them what I truly believed God had shown me. When they returned home that night and heard my message, they were amazed! Nothing had been in the prayer request that would give any clues as to the problem, and yet God revealed the problem and solution in my prayer time.

* * *

Another time, an urgent prayer request was sent out. Again, in prayer, the Holy Spirit took over my prayers and God revealed the key to the problem. I kept pressing in and again; when I felt God was done, I got up off my knees and thanked God for helping me. I believe it was a week or two after I was talking to the request-maker and told him what was revealed to me in prayer.

With amazement on his face, the gentleman said, "Nobody knew about this; how did you know that was the actual source of the problem?" My God is faithful, and His word is true!

* * *

At my church, we sometimes will have Prayer and Praise nights. One particular night, the prayer team was waiting in designated areas so if someone wanted prayer they would know where to go. A lady came up and asked for prayer; the elder got her permission to anoint her with oil. Carol, one member of the prayer team, prayed, then another team member prayed, and as she was doing that I was praying in the spirit quietly to myself. This lady wanted us to pray that God would help her to get pregnant, since she and her husband had been unsuccessful for 2 years. God told me to put my hand on her stomach and pray, and as I did, I could actually feel things moving. It was if God was cleaning up and putting things where they should be in order to answer her desire for a baby. She thanked us as we hugged, and off she went.

Four months later we had another one of those evenings and the same lady came up to our group again. This time we asked what she needed prayer for and she told us, with a big grin on her face, that she was there to praise God and to let us know she was pregnant. Is God faithful or what?

* * *

I guess it was three years ago. I got upset with one of the property managers where we live. I came home and informed my husband that I was fed up with things around here, and thus we should put our place up for sale. He just looked at me and said nothing. The next day, I actually went looking at an area that I had heard good things about, found a house, and made arrangements to see inside. While going through the house and checking out the backyard and swimming pool, I had all sorts of what I thought were "God ideas" for the new home. I was willing to give up what we had in our home and start over with this new house if this was what God wanted us to be doing. I think a few weeks went by, and I really felt like this was what God wanted; I wanted to meet with my pastor to inform him of what God had been showing me with this house. I felt I needed to talk to him to explain since my visions were about water baptizing in the swimming pool and I didn't want the pastor to have any wrong thoughts about it. I went to the appointment a bit early so I would have time to go into the sanctuary and pray about this meeting. I walked back and forth across the front of the church praying, and then the spiritual praying started. Once I felt there was nothing left to be said, I sat down and was quiet. Like the Word says, *"Be still, and know that I am God"* (Psalm 46:10).

Out of nowhere I heard, "I didn't tell you to move."

I still had my meeting, and yet I wondered, *Why did I go through all these weeks to end up with this conclusion?* Pastor Chris and I talked, and I asked him why he thought this might have happened. He turned it around, asking me if I had any idea.

Well, the one thing that did come to me was, I sometimes wonder how far I would go for Jesus. I couldn't see myself as a missionary in some third-world country, but what would I be willing to do for His kingdom? I truly felt like in the end, I was willing to give up my home—fully renovated, solid oak kitchen, marble tub inlay, good roof, etc.—and move to a house which would need renovations, with a plastic tub inlay, a regular kitchen (and a small one at that), and smaller rooms. But it had a swimming pool, which would be ideal for water baptisms. I think water baptisms are important; after all, Christ was water baptized. But God knows the future, and even though I was willing to go the mile for Him, Christ knew the financial bind we would be in down the road.

You see, a few months later Matthew had a stroke and didn't work again. What would we have done in this new situation? I believe God was pleased when He observed my willingness, but loved me enough to save me from the financial hardship.

There are so many other experiences I could share but if I did so, I would never get this book finished!

Absolute Solution

Thank you Holy Spirit for showing the way
How I should pray everyday
Pray to the Father with absolute confidence
Relaxed in His love and not desperate and tense.
When I pray from a position of knowledge, "it's
    mine"
This is what is taught, in Luke 18 verse nine
When the desire cometh, it is the tree of life
So why have deferred hope, sickness and strife?
You say, "Maybe prayer isn't the solution absolute"
Then give that devil of doubt the Royal Boot!
The Holy Spirit will tell you the things you should
    know
Then pray, have faith and God's glory He'll show.
My advice is very simple but true
The righteousness of God is in li'l' ol' you!
So clear your mind of the doubtful pollution
And know in your heart, prayer is the "Absolute
    Solution."

Trust and Obey

Isn't it amazing to think that God Almighty talks to us! But then, why wouldn't He? Our own earthly father talks to us, so why wouldn't our Heavenly Father? There are many scriptures that show us that God does in fact, talk to His children.

Shortly after accepting Christ, I shared with some people how I heard this voice telling me things, and how when I obeyed I would see fascinating results.

One gentleman, who had been a Christian for many years, surprised me when he told me, "I have never heard the voice of God like you do; I can't remember God ever telling me anything."

How does that happen? I wondered; I am nothing special. I suggested that maybe he did hear from God, and he just passed it off as ESP or a good idea he had.

I would like to share some of the conversations I have had with God, or perhaps I should say, which God has had with me.

I remember sometime in June, almost five years ago now, there was a special speaker at our church, Eastdale Christian Outreach Centre in Woodstock, Ontario. He was interesting enough, but what will always stand out in my mind is when Pastor Paul asked for a love offering for the speaker. I had just come back from holidays in my hometown, Brockville, Ontario, so needless to say, I didn't have much money in my wallet.

I started to hear this soft voice saying, "Give it all." I had only six dollars and change to last me until payday, and that was a week away. I gently refused with what I thought was a legitimate excuse, but again I heard, "Give it all." I quickly came back with, "I'll give two dollars; that will still leave me four dollars for the week."

The voice reassured me with, "Give it all; I will take care of it." After hearing this for about the third time, I figured God knew more than me, so I put in the whole six dollars and left my financial situation up to Him.

At the end of the evening the pastor ended with, "Whatever comes your way this week, turn it around to glorify God."

I went to work the next day—the two to ten shift. The first time in my four years of working as management with Tim Hortons, I received a phone call from an in-town manager. She was need of a midnight baker. I told the manager that we didn't have one in, and proceeded to inquire about the bake. When she said it was a forty-five pound bake plus the small cake donuts, I chuckled and offered my services. She was concerned about me being too tired for a midnight shift after just doing a shift of eight hours. I assured her I would do just fine, and I would tell her about it later. Well, I praised God and looked up with a smile and told Him He was amazing! I did my tills and made sure everything was all right for the midnight shift coming in; then I quickly left for home to change into my whites and go to the other Tim Hortons.

I was thinking about how the pastor had ended the service. This was nothing but God keeping His promise to me because I was obedient. But, did you notice: God didn't give up his insistent request because He already knew He had a blessing for me, and nothing was going to prevent His will for me being done. I could slap myself now with a wet noodle for not agreeing to put in the six dollars the first time I heard the voice. Being new at all of this, I had first questioned where the voice was actually coming from. After all, I am just Brenda Bates, a new little Christian, and the God of the universe is going to talk to me?

When I showed up for my shift, the Assistant Manager couldn't get over how refreshed I looked and so bubbly. She couldn't find a muffin person, so she had to do a double shift too. She looked and felt like she should go to bed. I did my bake, sang praises to God and talked to Him, and enjoyed myself back in my little kitchen. Customers really got their money's worth when they purchased my donuts, because I prayed an anointing all over the donuts.

Here comes the good part! The bake was over, the kitchen was scrubbed and clean, and then I went into the office.

The Assistant Manager remarked how good I still looked, and that opened the door for me to share with her why. She sat and listened as if hearing this kind of stuff for the first time. Are you ready for this? In the Bible it says to give God ten percent; I gave God six dollars on the Sunday night, and on Monday night, about twenty-five hours later, He sets me up to receive His promise and I got paid sixty dollars. I believe that was a pretty good return on my money, don't you?

* * *

Another night in church, I was going to put five dollars in the offering. When I opened my wallet, my eyes first fell on a ten-dollar bill. I felt "warm fuzzies" prompting me to put the ten dollars in the bucket when it was passed to me. God had that all planned too! I say that because of what had happened just previous to this night.

Friday, at the end of my shift, the schedule at work had to be changed because the other Assistant Manager noticed there was no baker for Monday morning. She asked me to fill in as baker, and decided to call someone else to come in and do the office work. On Monday, I came in with my whites on to bake, but then the regular baker came into the kitchen to bake too. Well, we were all a little confused. He offered to go home, but had to stay, since Sandra had phoned in at five a.m. to say that she was too sick to come to work. That put me in the office to do the administration work that day, after all.

On the desk was a note from the afternoon assistant stating that two purses had been handed in. She'd been too busy to call these women to let them know, and asked if they could be called on my shift. This is a policy we have, which saves people a lot of anxiety and phone calls.

I did the usual duties for that time of morning and then I called these ladies, being the "bearer of good news." The first lady was relieved, and I wrote down her address to make arrangements for Purolator to pick up and deliver the purse to her. The next lady was Greek, and very excited with my news. Quickly, she inquired whether her passport was in the purse; I put her mind at ease with a positive reply. I opened her wallet and tell her the sad news that there was no money, but at least all her credit cards seemed to be there. She directed me to a little zipper by the credit cards and gave me permission to open it. As I was doing so, I remarked with a chuckle how funny it feels to go through someone's wallet while talking to them on the phone. I was happy for her because I found two hundred dollars in fifties, and she told me that was exactly the amount she had in her wallet.

"Praise the Lord, they are all there!" I told her. Graciously, she told me to take one of the fifties and put it towards my Christmas. I refused, telling her that I was just doing my job by letting her know her purse was safe.

She insisted, and after about three or four times of her telling me to take the fifty dollars, I heard this voice saying, "Take it so she will be blessed." I thanked her and told her how much her generosity touched me.

Does this not blow you away? I mean, just think:

- I gave ten dollars instead of five dollars, and got fifty dollars.
- We missed the fact there was actually a baker booked to work.
- I got to work in the office after all because the office girl was sick.
- The afternoon assistant was too busy to phone.

Again, a pretty good return on my obedience. God is a rewarder.

Please don't get me wrong; God doesn't just think about money. He has many types of blessings for us, and amazingly, all were planned before we were even born! Sure, He knows what we want or need, but think of the joy you have when you are able to supply your child's desire when they let you know there is something that they would really like. Well then, shouldn't our Heavenly Father get the same thrill? Another thing: if He just gave us everything we asked for, then to whom or to what would *we* give? If we are specific in our requests to God and we receive them, then it builds our faith higher each time it happens. Therefore, God and all of us benefit.

I know from experience that if there is something God wants to accomplish, He will get it done by using someone else, if we won't listen.

* * *

One weekend, Peter Youngren was speaking on a Friday evening, then again on Saturday, after breakfast downstairs at the church. I went to listen and soak in the Word of God. The Friday night service was really good! On Saturday, as I entered the breakfast area, I was drawn to this table where three women were sitting. Two of them I didn't know, and the other I had only seen in church. We got to talking and joking. I made some remark that I had almost gone up front last night for a healing for my speech problem—I couldn't speak in tongues—but decided not to after all. The familiar lady said I should have. After the washroom parade, I was one of the last ones getting to the sanctuary. As I stood at the doorway I heard a voice telling me where to sit.

"Go and sit beside the woman you had breakfast with"; sure enough, there was a spot between her and another lady named Grace who went to my church.

During the sermon, God told me, "Ask her to pray for you." I knew He didn't mean Grace, so I apologized and told Him, "I couldn't; this is kind of personal and I don't even know her name."

I knew this lady could pray in the Holy Spirit, because I had heard her many times in church and wished I could do even half of that. Anyway, God kept gently prodding me to ask her, and I kept coming up with the same excuse why I couldn't. I did apologize to God for not doing as He asked me, but I felt I had a good reason and it wasn't because I was being stubborn!

The closing remarks indicated that the service was over and we would leave a much different person then when we came.

I stood and said, "Goodbye, I'll see you in church tomorrow, eh?"

As I turned to walk away I heard, "Yes, I'll be here." Then there was a touch on my shoulder, and she asked me if I had a minute.

I turned back to face her and replied, "Sure, what's up?"

This woman, Heather, informed me that while the service was on, God had told her to pray for me. I sat down, leaned over the chair ahead of me, and started to chuckle.

I thought to myself, *I don't believe this.* I told her about my conversation with God while the service was going on. Needless to say, she and one of the other ladies with her laid hands on me and started to pray, with my permission. I don't know just how long they had prayed. Then the Holy Spirit seemed to take over me and I freely slouched over on her. She kept backing up as she guided me to the floor. When I opened my eyes I chuckled, because I felt different. I knew my prayer for my Heavenly language had been answered. As I stood, Heather told me to open my mouth, speak my new language, and not to be disappointed if it was only a few words at first. Well I tried, I did, and I was excited, because God had heard me and made sure that I would receive my gift that day, even if I was too shy to ask for prayer.

I drove home, not even feeling the car seat under me, and praising God for my gift from Him. I wrote the events down in a book and then stood with hands open, waiting for another word or two. I stood like that for a time telling God, "I don't have to go to work until tomorrow, so I will wait on You."

I received a few more words, so I decided to go for a walk down by the water. I practiced my new language all the way there. I felt like I was flying home as I kept practicing my precious words!

I used to pray, "If it is Your will, can I pray in tongues; will you give me the language?" Then Pastor Paul's wife, Lisa, showed me in the Bible that it is God's will that we all speak in tongues. The Holy Spirit is a gift, according to Acts 2:38, one that enables us to speak even though we don't know what we are saying. But guess what? The devil doesn't know either; therefore he can't interfere or interrupt the plans of God.

Later on, whenever a situation comes up and goes remarkably well, it will blow your socks off when you realize that this must have been the reason why you were led to pray in the Holy Spirit.

* * *

One Sunday afternoon, we were heading for London when a winter storm picked as we were approaching the 401 from the on ramp. The visibility was so bad that I was forced to lower my speed to 20 kilometers per hour.

I seriously thought about turning back, but something inside reassured me that God was watching over us. Philippians 4:6-7 says, *"Be anxious for nothing, but...let your requests be made known to God"* (NKJV). I kept praying for protection and relying on Him to get Larry, my stepson, back home. I found myself praying in the Holy Spirit and believing that the weather conditions would improve. God did not put us out here on this highway for something bad to happen, so in the name of Jesus, I commanded the weather to improve. I think it was only ten minutes into our drive when the rain seemed to let up and the winds died down. Praise God, it cleared, the rest of the trip was fine, and the speed limit was safely reached. It was amazing to witness the difference in the weather within ten to fifteen minutes.

* * *

Another time at work, I started to hear God's voice. At least, I thought it must be, because I wouldn't have those kinds of thoughts on my own, and the words kept coming. While I was working, I would still pay attention to what He was saying so that I could write it down. It was just a simple message He was giving me. He had a word for the church I used to go to as a child back in Brockville. God ended that conversation with, "Tell Maureen that she doesn't have to go to England; her mother is going to be OK."

When I got home, I called the minister in Brockville and told him what I had heard at work. We had only met me once before, but he agreed to look up what the word for the church was, and let me know. Before hanging up, I mentioned God's message for Maureen and he said he would pass it on even though he knew nothing about any problem. I assured him that I didn't either, but this is what God wanted Maureen to know.

I was praying and singing on my way to Brockville after being told that I would be able to share with the congregation that Sunday. Apparently, he had checked with one of the older members of the board, who just happened to have been my favourite Sunday School teacher. She felt the church body would have no problem with what I had shared with him. I had also been praying that the minister wouldn't have a lengthy sermon, so that I would not be taking away from his time. Well, I called him when I got to my mom's home, and made arrangements to meet with him just before the service started. We got together and he admitted that try as he might, he didn't really have a sermon ready. I kind of chuckled and told him that I had been praying. It sounded like God had answered my prayer. We chuckled a bit and then we prayed for the service.

Before leaving he mentioned, "By the way, just after we hung up the other day, Maureen came to my office. She was all upset and didn't know what to do about her mom. She didn't know if she should go to England or trust God to look after things." Maureen had just returned home from England, and had her job to get back to. "I had the privilege of telling her the message God gave you for her. This is truly amazing! "

See how God looks after things? How important it is to listen, to be obedient, and not let the devil convince you that you don't hear from God! By sharing that message about Maureen, he was able to give her peace of mind.

I was somewhat nervous about the song I sang before I spoke, "I am Trusting in You." This song was recorded by the Neilsons, a family group who sang at my church in Woodstock (whom God blessed by financially supporting their album recording earlier in this book). It really ministered to me and I felt that this was the song for Brockville. God is so good! I actually got to meet the man who wrote that song a few weeks later. After my introduction, I proceeded to tell the congregation how God had given me a word for the church. When church was over, one lady specifically came over and told me that the word was definitely for her, and thanked me.

* * *

God's timing is everything, as you will find out at the end of this account.

I had an appointment for therapy at the hospital one day. I took the usual route, but for some reason, something made me stop in to check out the chapel. I looked around at the small but cozy room, and when I looked at the front, words that I wasn't thinking or planning on saying just came out.

"Lord, let Mom know You are with her today; thank you," I said, and with that I went on to my appointment.

That night, after supper, I called my mom just to talk, like I did just about every night. She told me that she had driven Joyce, her friend, to Toronto for a dentist appointment, and they had stayed overnight. It was early that morning when they set out for home. The day was beautiful! Joyce didn't want to drive because of the medication she had to take and her mouth was still quite sore. All was going well until just the other side of Belleville, when, all of a sudden, a freak white-out happened. Neither of them could see the road in front of them. They partly rolled down the windows in the small white car, hoping at least to see the yellow line on the side of the road. There was no way they could see the white line in the middle of the road. Out of nowhere came a whoosh and then another one, and as they looked up, they saw the tail lights of two semi transports. This white-out lasted only a few minutes, but thank God He was with them! They were on a two-lane highway when two transports had come up on them. With a transport on each side of them, they were amazed that an accident hadn't happened!

My mouth dropped as I listened to my mom tell me about this potentially fatal situation. I started to get a bit emotional and she asked me what was wrong. I proceeded to tell her of my experience in the chapel, and how God had put those words in my mouth. Are you ready for this? At the same time as I was in the chapel, my mom was in the white-out on Highway 401. Is God faithful or what?

My lesson in this is: when God puts someone or something on my heart to pray for, I do it! He knows far more than I do; I don't question why or what, I just pray. You notice it wasn't a long, drawn-out prayer either, just short and sweet and to the point. God likes it simple!

* * *

You know, we serve an amazing loving God who truly does care about every aspect of our lives. He has a way of opening doors so that we can be blessed and/or get an answer to a prayer or a concern.

I remember one time, while living on my own, I went to the bank to deposit a cheque along with $50. I put both on the counter in front of the teller and proceeded to read some wall signage while she did her thing. She noticed I had reversed a number on the cheque amount and asked me to initial the correction, then asked me for the $50. I was surprised, because it was there with the cheque and deposit slip, and now she was saying she didn't have it! I tried to stay calm—I emptied my wallet, purse and pockets in front of her and another staff member. Still no $50. I did the same thing again in front of another staff member, with no positive results. The teller told me that she would be right back. She was going to go down the hall and count her till. It should be no problem since the bank had only been open for forty-five minutes and it wasn't overly busy, so I thought. She came back and said that her till balanced; this I could just not understand.

The bank manager came out, and after getting all the details, he looked at me and said, "All the procedures were done correctly, but we will check again at the end of her shift and call you if we find the $50."

I left so frustrated and upset; fifty dollars was a lot of money to me. To make a long story short, the money never showed up in her till. I went to the only other store I was at that morning and they pulled their till and there was no extra money. I truly didn't think there would be, since I knew in my heart the money was at the bank. I did contact customer service at another TD bank, and questioned the agent on the procedure. She informed me that because the bank is insured, they should have given me back my money. I don't know what she did after the phone call, but several weeks later, I received a questionnaire from TD banks.

This is too funny, I thought, since the only thing left I had there was my student loan account. I did fill it out because the lady who looks after school loans is really nice and I wanted to give her a good review. "Something" made me also jot down the situation with the $50 quickly. Then I closed the envelope and mailed it off. In a few short weeks, I received a phone call from the bank thanking me for filling out the questionnaire.

The money situation was brought to the attention of the same bank manager at the time. Would you believe it—since I had been consistent in my complaint about the money and was still understandably upset, the manager was going to put the money in my account. Praise God! I believe it was God who prompted me to jot down the $50, because I was getting ready to seal the envelope without doing it. See how God looks after the situation when wrong has been done to one of His children? I am still in awe of that!

* * *

I know God uses us to fulfill what He wants accomplished. I had not been attending Eastdale Christian Outreach Centre for very long when it happened. There was an invitation for mothers to come forward for hands-on prayer at the front of the church. I went up with several others, but it felt like something was directing me to stand near a particular woman.

During the pastor's words that preceded the praying, I started to hear, "Put your hand on her back."

I could see exactly where I was supposed to put my hand. I heard this a few times and I hesitated; I told God that I was new here, and I didn't want anyone to think I was strange. The last time I heard the prompting, I did it. With that, the lady put her arm around my shoulder. We stood there together as the pastor came down, prayed, and laid hands on us as he passed by. When we turned to go back to our seats, the lady thanked me and told me that the moment I put my hand on her back, the pain went away. She had gone up for prayer for her back pain. Amazing how God does these things! What a blessing to be used—and He uses anyone who is willing. I usually still question the voice when I hear it, because I don't want to do anything that is not honouring God. If this happens to you, please don't disregard what you hear and think it couldn't happen to you. That could very well be a lie from the devil, because he knows exactly what can be accomplished when we are obedient to God's promptings.

I trust and hope that as you are reading these experiences of mine, they will excite you, motivate you to get into the Word, search God, spend time in His presence, and bask in His unconditional love. If you don't already have a relationship with Jesus, I encourage you to start one!

I had someone prophesy over me several years ago that I would, among other things, be like Ezekiel and speak over old bones (see Ezekiel 37). Maybe this is what this book is doing: speaking to people whose relationships with God have died out, gotten old and uneventful. Reading this book may encourage you to ask the Holy Spirit to bring that relationship to life again!

I think it is very useful to journal. We write down the great things God is doing with us or to others. When the devil tries to bring us down with his lies, we have the journal to go back to and be uplifted and refreshed. I know for me when I read over my notes, I experience those things all over again and my faith seems to get deepened and refreshed!

* * *

I was away on a trip during the time when I was wondering if Matthew was the man God wanted me to marry, so I asked God for a sign. I asked, "God, if you want me to marry Matthew, let him mention the time of year of our wedding." *This seems strange—why not the month?* I wondered. Those were the words that just came out, so that was how I left it. I thanked Him and prayed for a good trip back home from Florida.

I called Matthew when we got back to Woodstock, and we met for coffee. He brought me up to date about my dog and other things, and then he started on his second cup of coffee.

"I have been thinking, we should be able to get married by the end of summer or the beginning of fall; what do you think?"

I started to laugh and explained why, "I just asked God this morning for a sign if you were the one I was to marry, and you just provided the sign that I asked God for."

You know what is so good about this experience? In the future when life's issues throw a curve ball, we can stand firm! John 8:44 says that the devil *"is a liar and the father of lies."* God had Matthew planned as my husband from the very beginning of time. My marriage is covered in the blood of Jesus.

Principles of Prosperity

God will tell me what to sow
He's the One who's "in the know"
When I give with the right heart motive
The results can't help but be positive.
I sow and then stretch my faith for that seed
God always provides what I need.
Be smart, not like the man in Proverbs 28:22
Listen to God so this doesn't happen to you.
When I acknowledge Galatians 6:6-9
Then all God's promises will be mine.
You see, wealth doesn't come very fast
We should know that from the past
Give because God has stirred your heart
Then you're a guaranteed winner 'cause you've
    done your part.
God blesses us so others we can bless
This practice will keep us out of a financial mess.
When giving to God is our prime motivation
He will put us in a win/win situation.

Treasures in Jars of Clay

2nd Corinthians four verse six
Let the Light of God be your fix
Out of the darkness be His Light
So our futures can be so bright
We have treasures in our jars of clay
All-surpassing power of God throughout our day
We are hard-pressed on every side
But not crushed when in Jesus we abide
Remember when others speak in negative tone
Forgive, because we are never alone
Pray as we enjoy the treasures in jars of clay
Knowing our trial help mold us, God's way.

LIFE AFTER HOME CHURCH

You have been in the same church for what seems forever; you have a position, obligations and commitments. Years have created and developed many relationships, some closer than others, but there is a social circle you belong to.

What is with this feeling of soul-searching? It has come from somewhere but where? It is definitely spiritual, and seems to be eating away at you. You don't understand it and yet you keep going to church, praying, worshiping, listening to the sermon, but you leave feeling empty, repressed and upset because you don't know what the problem is. You really begin to question yourself, to investigate the motives or what you think are the motives behind this 24-7 feeling. You read the Word, do devotions, talk and pray to God daily and several times at that; yet there it is, eating away with great persistence.

How do you do it? Do you treat it like window-shopping? Do you check out other churches, or make an appointment with your pastor? You don't want to betray your home church, and my goodness, what will your friends think! You have heard how some people have been treated after they left. Pray, pray, pray, and then be silent?

"Be still, and know that I am God" (Psalm 46:10a).

How do you tell the pastor who has married you, baptized your children, been to your home for supper or the occasional BBQ, that you are not spiritually happy or satisfied at that church any longer? Your responsibilities have to be considered. Someone has to be carefully chosen to handle the duties and position. So many details to deal with, but I believe when you know it is God, God will take care of everything.

This happened to me a while ago, even though I knew inside I had to pray for the right person to take over the Resource Room for me. I'd held that position at my church since we started it five to six years earlier. I could not explain it at the time, but it was like God was letting me know He had other plans for me now. It finally happened; a young lady in the church had a dream about the Resource Room in which she was asked if she would be interested in the job. She had received confirmation that afternoon from someone else in the church. We talked, and it was definitely God.

Wow, freedom! Yet I was still asking God, "Now what do You want me to do?"

Eventually, a couple of things came up and I got involved. There were some meetings to attend to get the full picture and purpose of the Altar Ministry and to teach the New Believers class. I sat in all ten classes. I was so excited: finally I could do something in the church that would help new believers and be of service to others who went to the altar for various reasons.

With declining numbers needing altar assistance, I, along with others on the team, remained on our chairs more often than not. Near the end of my time at the church, I noticed that there were fewer invitations to come forward to accept Christ. The invitations were more geared toward asking the congregation to give to the new building fund. Sermons seemed to have more of a "tithe and offering" theme. There weren't enough new believers to form a new class, so I never had the chance to teach.

Even though these new challenges didn't progress, I am thankful I had that exposure. I will have that experience for the next road God puts me on.

As far as having a meeting with the pastor, I truly felt that at the time he wasn't going to change the course he was on just because of me sitting in his office telling him, "I am really feeling spiritually unsatisfied." So I prayed, then I would name a church and wait to see if God would somehow indicate that was where He wanted us to go. This went on for almost two years.

I have heard people say different times, "God directed me to this church," so I prayed and believed God would do the same for me. This is so important. I didn't want to just leave like others had. We'd gone through a lot of major changes in the church in a reasonably short period of time. Some left hurt, angry and feeling totally spiritually unattached.

To leave a church because you get a knot in your face, your feelings get hurt, you didn't like what the pastor said, or your friend got insulted or slighted and you took on their offense is just spiritual suicide. No church is perfect, no pastor is perfect, and they are human like all of us. They make mistakes like we do. You leave because you have prayed and waited for God to give direction. Why take useless baggage with you? Do you honestly think you will find a pastor who will always say what you want to hear, and that people are always going to be polite and treat you and your friends with the highest esteem? Hello, it doesn't happen!

So you pray for direction, like I mentioned before. That is how I came to the church we are attending now. When you have God's direction, you are in a place where you can receive what He has for you. I left work one day and something prompted me to pray about what church God would have us attend. I did just that; I stopped at one church my friend had told me about, sat in my car in the back parking lot, looked at the building, and waited.

"Home" is what I so softly heard. I just knew this was it. I was so excited, for finally the search was over, and I had this smothering heaviness lifted from me. Praise God! Now I asked God to reveal to Matthew, my husband, where we were to go to church. He was the head of the house and he would be the one to lead us to the place of worship. I never told him about my praying about the Innerkip church on my way home from work and sitting in its parking lot.

Two or three days after my encounter, out of the blue, Matthew asked, "Are we checking out that church here in Innerkip tomorrow?"

I innocently agreed with him and assured him how much Grace, Rick and Victoria enjoyed the pastor and the church body.

With great joy and expectation I got ready for church. For the first time in many months, I felt like a child on Christmas morning. As we came up the stairs inside we were greeted with warm, smiling faces and a sincere handshake. We were handed a bulletin and then we proceeded to sit in the same row where Grace and Victoria were sitting. This made me feel like I was at home.

The praise and worship songs were familiar from our last church, which again made it feel like home. I noticed the offering envelope, so I put the envelope I had filled at home inside it, and had it ready for offering time. Matthew also noticed the envelope on his side and showed it to me as he pointed to a little box in the corner and told me I should check it off.

"Please send me envelopes," is what it read. I leaned over and asked, "Does that mean we are coming here?"

He puckered his bottom lip and gently nodded.

"Praise God." He had put it in Matthew's heart!

During the sermon I heard a gentle voice say, "You have to tell Pastor Steve you are not going back."

The whole atmosphere made me feel like I was home. It was kind of like the Methodist church I attended while growing up. Would you believe the last hymn we sang was "Sinner Come Home, Jesus Is Gently Calling"?

That evening, I shared with Matthew about the day I had prayed as I drove to the back of Innerkip Presbyterian Church, and what I had heard there. I also mentioned how I had asked God to tell him where we were to go to church. I delicately showed him how God does speak to us and encouraged him that God did indeed talk to him. It was a really great experience.

Many weeks have gone by and I am already involved in some things at the new church. I am sitting on the edge of my chair, because I just know God is going to do some awesome things in that church with the ones who are obedient and wanting more of Him. This church may not be charismatic like the one we left, but the Holy Spirit is here and I can sense Him, see Him in others, and hear Him from the pulpit.

Considering everything, I truly believe this is where God wants Matthew and me. We are enjoying this church, and every Sunday I just can't wait to go.

I feel sad for others who don't go to any church because they have left their home church. For whatever reason, the hurt, the misuse of trust, and the realization that what is preached isn't necessarily practiced still affect a lot of people. How do we go about healing and getting back on track? How do we get to the point of letting ourselves trust a man of God again? Is our mindset to "throw out the whole bushel because there are one or two rotten apples"? Is this unrest and confusion the devil's dirty work, keeping God's people from being spiritually fed, blessed and fulfilled?

I also think some people use problems at church or the actions of church leaders as an excuse to leave, stay at home, and do their own thing. Instead of honestly admitting to themselves that they don't want to be bothered by God anymore and the whole church thing, they just blame the church leadership.

When I run into someone from the other church and we talk, it is like seeing an old family member. I remember one day I went to see an older couple from the other church. God had given me a poem about her, and I wanted to give it to her and visit with both of them. It was so good to see them again! She greeted me at the door with a big smile and a hug, which I did not let go of too quickly. I stood there and held this little Dutch lady and felt her love and warmth towards me. I walked into their living room and her husband stood up to greet me. We smiled and hugged, and again I could not let go. Then a flood of emotions came flowing from my eyes: I don't know just what order they came in, but there were great memories of our time with the Helps ministry, doing church in the hospital chapel, our meetings in homes, and things I had learned from him. Then I felt some sort of anger or frustration at the leadership of the church that caused people to leave. Why do things have to change and cause "families" to split up? How come the spiritual leaders don't take to heart the scripture Jeremiah 23:1-2, where God says `Woe to the shepherds who are destroying and scattering the sheep of my pasture"? After all, they know more and understand more of the Bible then we do; for some reason, we, as the congregation, expect them to act better. We forget they are only human and they still make mistakes but are those kinds of mistakes excusable, and if so, who gets to excuse them? Only God can truly heal our broken hearts and clear our confusion, and in time we can accept what has happened and go on as Christ would have us go on.

We must never quit praying for our pastors. The devil has an agenda and they are on the top of the list. There are so many questions, so many ways of looking at this sad situation of good people leaving their home church.

I trust that as you are reading this chapter, it will shed some light on this type of situation for you. If you have left a church and just never gone back, you are not an evil person, nor are you someone God no longer loves nor cares for. Please pray and find the church you know God wants you in. The Word encourages us to be in church, to worship together, and to fellowship one with another. We cannot do this on our own. *"But if we walk in the light, as He is in the light, we have fellowship with one another, and the blood of Jesus, His Son, purifies us from all sin"* (1 John 1:7).

Like my good friend Bruce R. once said to me, "It is so important to keep your eyes on the cross, not the leadership; that is the key."

There is life after leaving your home church. With God's continuous love, direction, and forgiveness, we can move on and do what He has planned for us. We owe it to Him, ourselves and others to fulfill the plan.

There is so much to this chapter a person could get into. I can only speak from my experiences.

Please, dear readers, Don't take this as a "slam the leadership" chapter because it isn't. They are only human and make mistakes. They need our prayers daily. "Higher level, bigger devil," I once heard someone say on TV.

As you read, if you find yourself in a similar situation, know you are not alone. Hopefully by the time you finish reading this book, you will be rejoicing for where you are now because of where you have been.

I think that is why it is so important to pray and seek God's direction. I can't help but believe that when He gives you direction and you obey, you will be blessed. We are blessed so we can be a blessing.

Being Blessed

I started a beautiful spring day by going a friend's home for prayers and devotions. Afterwards, over coffee, she mentioned the number of robins that were in her backyard that morning.

"Gee, I haven't seen one yet!" I mentioned to her. On my way home, I decided to take a path along the railroad and behind the motor homes instead of the entrance into the park. Remembering my time and conversation with my friend, I asked God if He could send a robin for me to see. As I walked, I sang to Him and enjoyed the warmth of the sun on my face. Upon approaching the corner of my home, I noticed a robin sitting on the grass. I hesitated for a moment, relishing in the fact that God just provided the answer to my request. Slowly, I started forward, and so did the robin. I was absolutely delighted as the robin walked instead of flying away, even though I was slowly walking behind him. We walked this way for the full hundred yards or so, and when he got to the gate he flew away. I sighed, walked through the gate, and came inside and called my friend.

"Hello Grace, you might have seen robins today in your backyard but God allowed me to walk with a robin on my way home," I said with teary-eyed excitement in my voice! When I hung up, I sat down and felt completely humbled to think that God would arrange that for me.

Being a Blessing

One morning I was busy downtown doing Welcome Wagon business. As I walked to my car after leaving the business of one of my sponsors, I noticed an older man trying to get a drink from the public fountain. It was very warm that morning and I could tell by his reaction that his attempt to get a refreshing drink wasn't accomplished. He muttered something as he proceeded to sit on the nearby bench.

I was rushed for time, but something made me go across the street to a restaurant to ask for a cold glass of water with ice if possible.

As I approached the stranger, I said, "I noticed you couldn't get a drink of water, so I got this cup of ice water for you."

He thanked me and I turned to say, "You are welcome and God bless you."

He seriously answered back, "God bless you!"

I walked on clouds back to my car, which was nearby. When I drove past that bench the man was gone; I couldn't see him anywhere as I drove down the street. I wondered how he could have disappeared so quickly, since he didn't seem to be a fast walker. Wow, to think God used me to give a stranger a drink...and then the Bible verse came to me. *"The King will reply, 'Truly, I tell you, whatever you did for one of the least of these brothers and sisters of mine, you did for me'"* (Matthew 25:40).

Being a Blessing and an Answer to Prayer

There was a new couple from out of town attending our church, after hearing about it and moving closer to Woodstock. The Welcoming Team asked the congregation if we would do a potluck supper for this couple. I offered to bring something, but didn't know exactly what. I could not help but feel like God was telling me to do a dish with shrimp. Shrimp is a little expensive, but if that is what God wanted me to bring then I would do that kind of dish. I later found out that I was the only one who had a shrimp dish, and apparently, anything with shrimp is the husband's favourite meal. Thank you, God!

Later on I found a place in London, Ontario, where I could take Portuguese lessons. My husband is from the Island of Pico, and it would be nice to be able to speak the language.

I was really looking forward to the first night of class, so in order not to be late I planned on having an early supper. I was cutting up celery when I heard God say, "I want you to give this new couple three hundred dollars."

Needless to say, I paused for a minute and asked if I had heard correctly.

God told me again, "I want you to give this new couple three hundred dollars."

Well, I was so at peace with this; I just knew it was God because on my own, I would never offer that much money to a couple I had just recently met. I wrote a cheque for them and put in my purse, thinking I would give it to them on Sunday. But God had a better plan!

I left early for class, and it is a good thing because I got lost, but not by much. The strange thing was that I didn't see anyone around when I did find the building. With much relief, I did see a secretary sitting behind her desk. She inquired as to why I was there. When I mentioned the Portuguese class, she glanced at her paper, and as she looked up at me she said, "Everyone was phoned to let them know that the class has been cancelled this week."

She confirmed that my name was on that list and that somebody had left me message. I'd missed the call because I left early for class.

"Well, I won't have to leave early next week for class now that I know where it is," I remarked with a grin as I said goodnight.

As I started for home, God reminded me of the cheque in my purse. He wanted me to take it to this couple on the way home since I go through their town. I checked my watch and thought it would not be the best time, since they would more than likely be having supper. Like I mentioned earlier, I didn't know this couple all that well. It had only been a few weeks since they started coming to church. I didn't want to be interrupting them, and couldn't see why I couldn't wait until Sunday. But God had put it on my heart that it had to be given that evening.

For a minute, I wondered if this was in fact why I had left early. God would have known the class was cancelled and that I would be driving through Thamesford, where the couple lived. Getting the phone call would have meant that I would have stayed home, but now I was able to be an answer to what turned out to be a desperate prayer.

I found the right home and knocked on the door. Though surprised to see me, the wife graciously asked me to come in. Her husband had just got in the door, and was washing up before supper. I declined the invitation to stay for supper, and with that I told them about the conversation God had with me earlier and that I was just dropping off this cheque.

She couldn't believe that someone who had only been a Christian friend for a short time would be willing to do this. They thanked me several times, and then we all agreed to give God thanks for providing. I was just beside myself as I drove home, to think God used me to accomplish His plan for this couple.

Sunday I found out something amazing!

The gentleman told me, "Before I left work that day, I received a phone call informing me that I had to have three hundred dollars by nine o'clock the next morning. I was desperate and cried out to God, where am I ever going to get that much money by morning? I hadn't gotten a chance to tell my wife about the phone call yet, and then you knocked at the door with an envelope and a cheque inside."

After hearing all of this, how I wished I could have seen the look on his face when he opened the envelope and saw the cheque for three hundred dollars! This is actual proof that God hears our prayers and that we hear His voice. Amazing!

I mentioned to him how I kept getting a sense of emergency on my way home: "My initial plan was to give you the cheque on Sunday, but driving home I really sensed that I had to give it to you on the way."

God is so faithful. He cares about everything that goes on in our lives. I am so thankful that I asked Him into my heart and that He is my Forever Friend, as we refer to Jesus in "Kid's Camp."

I love when He whispers things in my ear that He wants me to do. Don't get me wrong, I don't always hear clearly; sometimes I hesitate a bit before acting on it, and sometimes I miss it completely. When I realize my mistakes, I immediately ask for forgiveness and God is faithful—He forgives. God is also patient!

But most of all, in that quiet time, I am comforted when I just hear Him whisper, "I love you."

BEING BLESSED, JUST ASK

I remember one Sunday morning, sitting in church waiting for the service to start, when I was thinking for a moment about a couple who had just bought a new car. Then I felt a "drop" in my heart to ask God to put it on somebody's heart to buy Matthew and me a new car; we could really use one. I hesitated for a minute, asked for even a used car and then said, "No, a *new* car, thank you Jesus."

The service started and I didn't give that request another thought; I didn't even mention it to Matthew or anyone else. I guess it was about the middle of the week when I received a phone call from a lady whom I know very well. We did the usual small talk and then she informed me that she had just left the accountants' that afternoon and that she had to get rid of some money or she would be paying a lot of taxes. Praise God! She "thought" of Matthew and me, and she was going to be sending a cheque to buy us a new car. Well, it's not necessary to say what my reaction was! I proceeded to tell her about my quick request to God just the past Sunday morning. We bought the new car, paid off a small visa bill, and had money left over. For years I had always wanted personal license plates, because we bred Bichons and I thought it would be advantageous to promote that with the plates. I never did because in reality, it would be a luxury, and did I really need to have them? But with this new car, I immediately asked God what I could put on the plates that would glorify Him. I put out a few suggestions, but got nothing; then I just stood still and waited for an answer—after all, I had just asked God a question. Within a couple of minutes or so I heard "Prayed 4."

"Ok Lord, I will go tomorrow and order those," I told Him. I couldn't get over the peace and joy that came over me. To think, I was asking a question while standing in my driveway and God answered me, of all people, me...it humbles me every time I think about it.

I went in the next day to the Ontario Transportation Office and requested personal license plates with "Prayd 4" on them. The lady looked up something and told me that those license plates were already assigned. I was about to say, "I don't understand," when she told me to wait a minute. It seems Ontario plates were able to have another letter and so I got "Prayed 4" after all. I chuckled as I thanked her, and said that it was a good thing, since my Dad had told me specifically what to get.

Weeks later, when my pastor asked if I could share my story in church one Sunday, I said sure. The pastor half-jokingly (I think) asked, who else could pray for a car and have faith that she would get it but Brenda? As I finished, I believe the Holy Spirit stepped in with the closing remark, "Don't let the devil steal what God wants to give you anyway—ask!"

I could have thought, *Oh yeah, as if that would happen* and not have done it, but thank goodness I did. Those plates have been a testimony since 2003 when I put them on the car. Out of the blue, people would comment on the plates and of course I would tell them my little story. I have had people give me thumbs-up at the traffic lights and one day I found a note on my car from a fellow Christian lady who wrote that she really liked my plates. One thing I have to especially remember now is how I drive and my reaction to the way others drive, if you know what I mean. I sometimes laugh at myself when I think that people read those plates and figure I am the one who is prayed for if I make a mistake while behind the wheel.

I am just a normal person, but God blesses His children in so many ways! He is looking for willing and open people. He loves to bless His children, and the best example is John 3:16. If as parents we enjoy it when we can bless our children, think then how much more God enjoys it. That also is scriptural!

Whispers

O Lord, how I appreciate
That You would talk to me,
Please give me Samuel's ear
Alert and quick to hear.
Forgive me if at times I hesitate
When I hear Your call...
At times it amazes me
That You would talk to me at all!
Thank You for Your Forgiveness
Your Mercy and Your Love
Thank You for Your Whispers
That come from You above,
So, no matter day or night
And I hear You call my name
May I reply, "Here I am Lord
Fill Me with Your might
So when, I hear You whisper Lord,
I will always do what is right."

Pray and Watch

Yes, you have to do your part
But did you ask Him where to go?
I find on my own I'm not that smart
Ask then listen, He will let you know.
We try so hard to do it on our own
Because we know what is at stake
But through history this has been shown
It ends up as a big mistake.
You know the excitement that you feel
When skiing down that great big slope
The same is when you realize God is real
And in Him there is always Hope.
You have to open up your heart
Willingly, get on your knees
Pray and ask God to do His part
Then watch what you will see!

I Fall in Love

I fall in love with Jesus more each day
As I learn of His loving way
It's more than dying on Calvary
And rising again on day three.
It's how He speaks softly in my ear
Or says something kind to wipe away a tear
It's feeling the warmth, being wrapped in His arms
And knowing His presence keeps me from all
   harm.
The confidence of walking hand in hand
Knowing all things are done at His command
Giving me wisdom in what I should speak
And showing me things as I eagerly seek.
O, to know I am never alone
Daily, His love for me is shown
He's not just my Saviour and Lord, He's my Friend
With a friendship with Jesus, there is no end.

The Light

How long do I have to be in this tunnel?
This tunnel with no end
Isn't there somebody out there
That has some encouragement to send?
I'm doing my best to cope with the dark
But God, I really need some little spark.
This tunnel is dark, damp and full of gloom
How I long to see the flowers in full bloom.
Pray and put my faith to the test
God can take care of the rest...
Suddenly, at the end of the tunnel
I saw something so bright!
No, it wasn't a train but Jesus Christ
For the world's darkness, He is the only Light.

SHE EMBRACES

Embraces her identity in Christ knowing she is loved, accepted, secure, and significant in Him!

Wow, I could never have said that, let alone believed it, before May 2, 1993.

Since I went to Sunday school as a child and then to youth group, I knew that God answered prayers, but I figured I could look after things myself. I am ashamed to say that I went to youth because, well, there were boys there, and it got me out of the house. But take things seriously?

As an adult, I made so many wrong choices and mistakes while looking to be loved and accepted.

I am so thankful I went down by the water after work one afternoon where God spoke and told me, "Tonight you should be in church."

You may remember, though I am somewhat embarrassed to admit it, that I asked if it was really God or my dad—he had died in August of the previous year, and he was a Christian. When I heard it again, well, that night I ended up in a church I had previously just heard about.

I accepted Christ that night. I had tears running down my face while I asked God to make me like Jesus. I remember saying that seven times. I have never looked back. Do I stumble? Yes, and God is there to pick me up, clean me off, and carry on with me.

It totally amazes me to look at my past with the realization that He was watching me all my life; seriously, it makes me cry like I am doing at this moment. He still loved me—me, can you imagine?

The more I get into the Word and read His promises, the more I'm amazed at the number of verses that state how much He loves us. I didn't know anyone who would die for me—ah, but I do now!

I experience so many of the things that are written in the Bible; how can I not believe the Word and tell others what a difference Jesus is doing in me, and how God can help them too?

Before, I didn't like the person I saw in the mirror: I had an inferiority complex big-time, I put myself down before anyone else could, and I felt like I was going through life without purpose.

The devil likes to keep us in that frame of mind, but the Blood of Christ erased those thoughts and took the devil's power away. The devil tried to convince me one Sunday morning to leave church, making it sound like the sermon was going to be like a boring history lesson. I almost got up, but something kept reminding me of how I would feel if I was speaking and someone got up and left.

Well, Praise God I stayed! Brett Andrews, who was filling in for our pastor, had an interesting message but at the end he asked us, "Do you know that God loves you and He believes in you?"

What? We are supposed to believe in Him, not the other way around! I was stunned to hear that. I was so awed by that question that I couldn't get it out of my mind the rest of the day. I started to get words that expressed what was going on in my heart. I will close with that poem, which has convinced me that I am significant in Him, I am secure in His love, I am accepted, and He believes in me.

He Believes In Me

Thank you, Lord, for changing my heart
And giving me a brand new start
Thank you for today, for You helped me see
That You actually do believe in me.
Never heard that in the past
What a revelation to receive at last!
At times when I think I can't get things done
I'll remember You fought the fight and won.
Whenever I am feeling down
You pick me and wipe away the frown.
But Lord, it truly is amazing
With a past I had just a blazing
You picked me to believe in
Cleaned me up and forgave my sin.
Please continue to give me Your character and
    integrity
Help me to live up to Your belief in me
Jesus, this is my cry, no, it is a must
That daily, I would be covered in Your dust.

About the Author

I am one of six children born to Orine (Bob) and Joyce Bates of Brockville, Ontario. At a young age, I started writing poetry for special occasions or if there was something on my heart that I wanted to express to someone. Sometimes it would be a poem to God. My Nanny Olla and my Aunt Alice both used to write poems, and would read them to me or give them to me to read. I truly enjoyed poetry, and as Head Girl of Brockville Collegiate Institute, I read a poem, "You Mustn't Quit," instead of giving a speech at commencement.

It wasn't until I accepted Christ, on May 2, 1993, that I realized that even though I was sinning all those years, God loved me and would answer my prayers. I was amazed that some of the thoughts I had would actually come to reality.

As I familiarized myself more with the Word and the Holy Spirit, more lines of communication opened up. How exciting that was for me! I sincerely encourage you to get yourself lined up with the Holy Spirit. The Spirit is a gift from God and He wants you to have it—the Word says so. It empowers you with God's presence. I am never alone; He comforts, encourages, and loves me, and when I don't know exactly how to pray, He helps me with that also.

I trust that as you read this book you will feel stronger in your faith, you will have open dialogue with the Holy Spirit, and, most of all, you will be sure that your salvation is secure and that nothing is impossible with God!